IMAGINE ALL THE PEOPLE

Imagine All the People

A Conversation with

the Dalai Lama

on Money, Politics, and
Life as It Could Be

His Holiness the Fourteenth Dalai Lama
and Fabien Ouaki

in collaboration with Anne Benson

Wisdom Publications • Boston

Wisdom Publications
199 Elm Street
Somerville, MA 02144 USA

Library of Congress Cataloging-in-Publication Data
Bstan-'dzin-rgya-mtsho, Dalai Lama XIV, 1935–
    [La vie est à nous. English]
    Imagine all the people : a conversation with the Dalai Lama on
money, politics, and life as it could be / His Holiness the Fourteenth
Dalai Lama and Fabien Ouaki in collaboration with Anne Benson.
        p. cm.
    Includes index.
    ISBN 0-86171-150-5 (paper : alk. paper)
    1. Buddhism--Social aspects--Miscellanea. 2. Religious life-
-Buddhism--Miscellanea. 3. Religion and politics. 4. Buddhism-
-Doctrines. I. Ouaki, Fabien. II. Benson, Anne. III. Title.
BQ7935.B774L3513 1999
294.3'4--dc21   99-11860

ISBN 0-86171-150-5

04 03 02 01 00
6   5   4   3

Set in Adobe Weiss and Garamond fonts, 11.5 on 16 point.
Designed by: Cynthia Dunne
Front cover photo: Clive Arrowsmith

Printed in the United States of America

Table of Contents

Prologue   vii

The Conversations

Power and Values   1

Global Community   21

Economics and Altruism   41

A Middle Path   65

Living and Dying   81

Mind and Miracles   111

Epilogue   139

Appendix: *The Global Community and
     the Need for Universal Responsibility* 141

Glossary   163

Index   171

About the Contributors   179

About Wisdom   180

Prologue

When you don't believe in coincidences, it is easier to sense why certain people you meet take on cardinal importance in your life. One evening in 1980 I visited a friend who was working at Europe 1, a French radio station. He had set up a studio in his home and was training radio announcers. That night I met three people who had started the first pirate radio station in France, called "Radio Here and Now." This station was an open forum, introducing broadcasting concepts that were unknown in France at that time. Little did I know how much that evening would impact my young life, and how it would eventually be instrumental in the creation of this book. One of the men I met that evening was partly responsible for bringing several Tibetan Buddhist masters to France. He casually mentioned that his teacher, Kalu Rinpoche, was giving a teaching in Paris. I decided to go to the event.

Kalu Rinpoche was old, thin, and apparently very frail, but he managed to infuse his surroundings with powerful feelings of love and compassion. He was kind, but quite distant, as if to say, "I love you, but I don't need anything. Don't become attached to me." He seemed to have no personal goal, but taught in response to the increasing number of requests from Westerners of all ages who were attracted to Tibetan Buddhism. That evening Rinpoche was giving an initiation related to Chenresig, the *bodhisattva* of great compassion, introducing the audience to the path of altruism. Tibet's Dalai Lamas are recognized as human emanations of Chenresig, who is especially beloved in Tibet.

Kalu Rinpoche wanted to know if anyone in the audience wished to "take refuge." Taking refuge is a bit like making an agreement with the Three Jewels: the Buddha, the Dharma (Buddha's teachings), and the Sangha (the community of Buddhist practitioners). Taking refuge is an intimate, personal decision. The main vow one takes is to do no harm to others and, whenever possible, to act for the benefit of all sentient beings according to the path revealed by Shakyamuni, the historical Buddha. For most people, the decision to take refuge is the result of a deeply pondered reflection. But I took refuge ten minutes after entering the room. I was totally convinced that Kalu Rinpoche was an authentic embodiment of compassion. His presence hit me like a bolt of lightning.

Although it took me quite a while to realize the meaning of my commitment and to begin to wrap my mind around a religion I hardly knew at the time, I never regretted my decision. Nevertheless, I refuse to be called a Buddhist. The label doesn't suit me. My religious and ethnic interbreeding—half-Jewish on my father's side, atheist on my mother's, Catholic via my mother-in-law, and spiritually curious by nature—offers me total freedom. With no deep roots, I feel at home anywhere. And yet I do believe that humans are more than makeshift packets of molecules. This "more," which the Jews call The Eternal Father, the Christians name The Lord, the Muslims call Allah, and the Buddhists define as the nature of mind, is the root of my faith, the thread I have been unraveling for so many years.

My first encounter with the Fourteenth Dalai Lama, Tenzin Gyatso, came about thanks to a Tibetan acquaintance of mine, one of the few Tibetan refugees the French government welcomed to France in the 1960s. This Tibetan was living with a childhood friend of mine, and I invited him to dinner. Over dessert he told me—in a highly confidential whisper—that the Dalai Lama would be spending an hour in the VIP transit lounge at Roissy Airport the following morning. "Would you like to meet him?" my Tibetan friend asked. Would I ever!

The next morning I slipped into the large airport salon. The Dalai Lama was comfortably seated, deep in conversation with someone I couldn't see. I sat down a few meters away, closing my eyes and settling into silence. Mustering all my powers of concentration, I started to mentally offer a *mandala* to His Holiness. Though neither assiduous in my practice nor proficient in traditional cosmogony, I knew a few things about this offering. I visualized a crystal clear sea in a world filled with soft, yet powerful light. Between sea and sky I added a few mountains. It was beginning to look something like a postcard.

Suddenly, from the depth of the picture, I saw the Dalai Lama walking toward me. Each step was punctuated by his deep, joyous laughter, and the sound swelled as he entered my field of vision. I opened my eyes, and there he was. His deep, joyous laughter rang through the air. I squeaked, "Fabien, you're dreaming!" But I was definitely awake—if not awakened.

Each of my next encounters with the Dalai Lama drew me closer to him. The religious and political leader of Tibet has long considered artists and the media more useful allies than politicians in disrupting the apathy toward the sufferings of the Tibetan people. As, among other things, a journalist and radio personality—as well as someone who strongly identifies with Tibetan Buddhism—I felt compelled to foster a relationship with His Holiness. During one of the Dalai Lama's rare visits to Paris, I arranged a meeting for him with a number of leading French artists and writers. This event coincided with the opening of a film I produced, called *Lungta*. The following year the Dalai Lama and I met again for the premiere of *Little Buddha.* In 1993 we worked together on a colloquium in which philosophers, businessmen, politicians, economists, and spiritual searchers shared ideas on business and ethics at the Palais des Congrès in Paris.

Subsequent visits with His Holiness piqued my interest, as well as my frustration. We never had enough time to discuss any subject in depth—until this book project. During a meeting we had in Marseilles, in September 1994, I explained to the Dalai Lama that I wanted to question him more deeply on ethics, business, global changes, the economy, personal relationships, and compassion in everyday life.

"Can this book help people?" he asked. "If so, let's do it! Prepare questions and I will do my best to answer." He was very happy to find another opportunity to communicate with the world. Faced with his buoyant enthusiasm, I began to wonder what I had got myself into. We arranged a series of interviews to take place in Dharamsala, India, at the Dalai Lama's residence-in-exile.

The best place to rent a jeep in Dharamsala is Nechung Monastery. Each day our chauffeur, a monk called Tenzin, picked us up at our hotel and dropped us off in front of His Holiness' residence, two kilometers up the mountain. As we were about to leave for our first meeting, the monsoon—several weeks late—decided to hit. In the twenty seconds it took to cross the garden, a dense fog gathered and a sudden shower drenched us. Amid fits of laughter, we crammed ourselves, our bags, and three open umbrellas into the jeep. A single windshield wiper flashed across the glass, utterly useless. Tenzin probably entrusted our destiny to his tutelary deity while the car cut a path through the opaque curtains of rain, sluicing across the thin, tortuous track leading up to the residence. I had visions of large slabs of road and mountain, parched by six months of drought and assuaged by such torrential rains, suddenly deciding to slide down the steep slopes to the foot of a neighboring cliff. My joy at the thought of meeting His Holiness shifted to panic. Fortunately, I didn't have much time to worry because the jeep had already pulled up before the gates of Thekchen Choling—the Mahayana Dharma Palace—the Dalai Lama's home. After the last furious gust of wind and rain ushered us into the security zone, the storm died out.

The Dalai Lama's bodyguards knew me. We had worked together on His Holiness' security team in Paris. Nevertheless, they inspected all our equipment before letting us pass through the gates. The palace is actually an old hillside residence dating back to English colonial times: a few low buildings surrounded by multiple gardens and steps that form a pleasant, but slightly mysterious labyrinth. Thousands of brilliant flowers had defied the downpour and a variety of birds sang sweetly. The walls of the waiting rooms and corridors were graced with the kindly gazes of painted buddhas and bodhisattvas. In the background one could hear deep, rhythmic chanting.

In the waiting room, I tried to collect my soaked possessions and scattered ideas. Luckily, I had prepared a list of questions that underlined the plan of the book. The first part would broadly address the state of the world. The second part would focus on individual problems and be an examination of everyday life. I thought this combination essential, because wisdom is not only for the clarification of fundamental questions, but should also retain a daily relevance. A third section would deal with natural and human mysteries. In this last part I would ask His Holiness questions about death, metaphysics, and the creation of the universe.

I jumped at the arrival of Tenzin Geyche, His Holiness' secretary. Our time had come? So soon? No, Tenzin Geyche had just come to say hello. While he discussed the details of my visit with my collaborator, Anne Benson, I plunged back into my notes, feverishly revising the day's plan. Finally Lhakdor, His Holiness' Tibetan-English translator, fetched us. We walked down the veranda, and there was His Holiness, standing before us. He seemed taller every time I saw him. He joyfully grasped my hand and pulled me into his private sitting room.

His Holiness likes to receive visitors and spend quiet afternoons listening to elderly Tibetans tell him even older stories in this well-lit, spacious room. A huge relief map of Tibet covers one wall, while a small altar with a beautiful statue and a *thanka* (scroll painting) of Chenresig occupy the opposite one. By the time I had extracted my notes and positioned the microphones, His Holiness was already happily seated in his armchair, facing the inner garden. Small talk has little place in His Holiness' vocabulary. We began straight away.

From July 10 to 16, 1995, Anne, Lhakdor, and I spent two wonderful hours each day with the Dalai Lama. Anne would transcribe the day's tapes every evening, comparing them with Lhakdor's notes the following day. My deep curiosity about life, as much as my attraction to Tibetan Buddhism and my respect for the Dalai Lama, provided me with inspiration throughout these interviews with His Holiness. I hope that the sense of spontaneity and joy, reflection and surprise that surfaced during these interviews surfaces again in *Imagine All the People*.

POWER AND VALUES

Power and Values

Fabien: Your Holiness, do you think it possible to introduce a system of laws, based on the Buddhist principle of interdependence, that would be more in harmony with human nature as well as modern, global society? Is it possible to create such laws without referring to a particular religion or philosophy?

Dalai Lama: From a Buddhist point of view, laws are a human creation. But then there are different systems. Some systems deliberately protect a single-party system—I am thinking of the laws set up by totalitarian regimes, communism in particular. Such legal systems go against human nature, and I personally think they are wrong. In democratic countries laws are also man-made, but their goal is to protect the rights and values of human beings. In general, I feel that laws should serve as guidelines for the proper use of human initiative, creativity, and ability.

Fabien: Do you think that democracy is helping laws to evolve in this way?

Dalai Lama: Yes. In democratic countries, legal systems should work that way and they generally do. But these laws nevertheless partially contradict the Buddhist principle of interdependence, since they do not include "democratic rights" for the environment and the animal realm. Most legal systems refer only to human rights and do not consider the rights of animals or other beings that share the planet with us. Laws that protect human rights and values and indicate proper ways to use human ability are not in contradiction with *karma* or causality—not in the Western sense where the same causes have the same effects, but in the Buddhist sense where each effect proceeds from a cause that also needs to be considered.

In reality, the problem is that for most "powerful" people there is a difference between the principle of the law and its application. Almost all legal systems condemn killing. This notion occurs in most countries of the world. Yet in practice, powerful people treat killing as they treat lying. For politicians, small lies are prohibited, but large lies are accepted. For a Buddhist this is a very obvious contradiction. The same applies to killing. When a man who is desperate kills another person, this small act is defined as murder. It is wrong. But the man who kills or gives orders to kill thousands of people is a hero! That is very unfortunate.

Most religious systems condemn murder, rape, and theft. In my opinion, religious principles are based on natural human attitudes and feelings. Their essential function is to inspire human beings to develop basic human qualities. Thus it seems logical that most laws would be consistent with the principles of positive karma. But in order for both religious and secular laws to conform to the principles of interdependence, we need to widen their perspective to include protection of the environment and the animal realm. This is how we can apply the Buddhist view of interdependence to a broader vision of law and order.

Fabien: What about money? Does money have its own intrinsic power? Do we have the means to control it, like we do laws? Is money a servant to higher motivations or has it become a god?

Dalai Lama: Let me say this: money is good. It is important. Without money, daily survival—not to mention further development—is impossible. So we are not even questioning its importance. At the same time, it is wrong to consider money a god or a substance endowed with some power of its own. To think that money is everything, and that just by having lots of it all our problems will be solved is a serious mistake.

In the Buddhist approach, worldly happiness is based on what we call the four excellences: the Dharma, wealth, *nirvana*, and satisfaction. Nirvana, or freedom from suffering, is the ultimate goal. The satisfaction achieved from a successful temporal life is just a transient goal. The teachings are the means to achieve ultimate inner freedom, whereas money and wealth facilitate worldly happiness, temporary satisfaction. One strives to achieve that which is positive for all beings. To do so, one must attend to both ultimate and temporary goals. Well-being and money belong to the latter category. In fact, Buddhist texts mention the fruition of eight qualities including wealth, health, and fame that define a "fortunate" human existence.

To enjoy even temporary happiness, however, one must first have peace of mind. Next comes health, then good companions, and then money, in that order, though of course all four aspects are connected. For example, when we had to escape from Tibet, our first priority was to save our lives. Being penniless was secondary. If one is alive, it is always possible to make friends and earn money. Peace of mind must come first. Peace of mind generally attracts prosperity. Certainly someone who has a peaceful mind will use his or her money judiciously.

The mind is key. If anything should be considered a god, so to speak, it is the mind, not money. A healthy, positive mind is the utmost priority. But if we were to reverse the order of these priorities, what would happen? I find it hard to imagine how a person with great wealth, bad health, no friends, and no peace of mind could feel even slightly happy.

Fabien: But many people live that way.

Dalai Lama: Yes, especially rich people like you! And then alcohol becomes their best friend, doesn't it? In the end, their fortune is exhausted and their health is spoiled. That is why someone who grasps peace of mind but not the other three elements can still survive and be happy, even in poor health. Inner peace alone can be enough to define happiness. Following the same logic, if you are in peace, healthy, and surrounded by trusted friends, surely you can survive without money. But reverse the situation and observe what happens. If someone has only money and not the other three elements, then they have nothing but problems. That is how I see it.

Fabien: Fine, but then how do you explain the importance that accumulating money has acquired in the modern world? For me, the present economic system is not intended to make people happy—its only goal is to make more money, to produce more wealth.

Dalai Lama: You are raising an essential point. It is a generally accepted principle in the West that for a country's economy to be healthy, the gross national product must increase every year. If it decreases, everyone panics. Something is wrong. Sooner or later we will have to change this archaic concept.

Practically speaking, I base my proposal to deal with this problem on the huge gap that separates the northern and southern countries. In Europe and other countries there is a production surplus, whereas the world's southerners are dying of starvation. Yesterday the BBC announced that one child in four in Somalia is starving. That is terrible. In India there are also many poor people.

Yet I must admit that I saw beggars even in the West! I was in Graz, Austria. I noticed a poor man sitting on a bench in front of the hotel where I was staying. The next morning when I looked outside, he was still there. He had slept on the bench. I felt very bad. We had eaten a good breakfast, and he had gone hungry. I sent the man some milk and bread through my bodyguard. He found out that the poor fellow was unemployed and had no home. One beggar in the West. That is quite sad. But here in India, there are hundreds of thousands of beggars.

Fabien: But what is your point of view, as a Buddhist, about money? I heard you don't touch money.

Dalai Lama: Why not? Of course I touch money!

Fabien: But I noticed that you don't open envelopes containing offerings.

Dalai Lama: That is because I give them to my office to deal with. I can touch money. The vows of a Buddhist monk clearly state that one should not touch gold. This is prohibited. But according to the bodhisattva practice, when someone offers you gold with a very sincere heart, if you refuse to touch it, that person may be disappointed. Under such circumstances even a monk is allowed to touch gold. The meaning of this vow is to reduce attachment.

The same applies to clothes. For example, a monk's robe is one of the thirteen articles, including his begging bowl, staff, and ground cover, that he may consider his own. If I happen to have extra garments—of course I have several—I can use them, but I am not allowed to consider them "mine." I must consider them as belonging to my abbot or someone else. These rules help reduce attachment. A monk is not permitted to claim ownership of anything except those thirteen articles. He must always maintain the attitude "This does not belong to me. I am only using it to serve others."

Such rules apply exclusively to monks and nuns, not all Buddhists. The vows we take on the day of monastic ordination involve three transformations: a change of attitude, a change of name, and a change of clothes. Since, from this day onwards, nirvana becomes our main goal, we must change our mental attitude and direct all our energy toward that. The question of survival is solved by begging for alms. We call this "equalizing merit." Whatever you get, you accept. Monks must eat their meals after the sun rises and before it crosses its zenith. No solid food is taken in the afternoon. The main purpose of all our vows is to reduce attachment.

Fabien: But what about attachment to money in general, lay terms? People usually consider their money their personal property.

Dalai Lama: Let's look a bit closer. I think there are two types of attachment or desire functioning here. Generally speaking, I have several thousand dollars at my disposal. In a certain sense, I feel this money is "mine." That does not mean, however, that I may use it to buy food, clothes, or anything else for myself. This money is spent on projects to help others. When I receive a donation from a Tibetan of one hundred thousand rupees, for example, I feel happy. I think, "Now I've got some money!" Some notion of desire may arise in me, but it is not for anything personal. I receive an allowance for my personal sustenance from the Indian government and collect some interest on personal, invested funds. I use the latter when I want to buy a watch or something personal, but I am very careful to spend donations, especially those made on behalf of sick or dying persons, entirely on spiritual or educational goals. There may be some desire in such circumstances, but it is not mixed with personal attachment.

Now let's consider the case of a company that makes lots of money. If those profits were used for community development projects or for helping people in need, and not necessarily consumed in the name of a luxurious lifestyle, that would be an example of "right desire."

Fabien: In my opinion, money is becoming a bit like the golden calf in the Bible. Is money just an image projected by our unceasing wants and needs?

Dalai Lama: Certainly not! For me, the story of the golden calf can symbolize the potential dangers of our attraction to money and our increasing desires when we replace God with a concrete object. As I said before, money is undoubtedly important. To tell you the truth, I even think that from a global perspective the amount of money produced in the world is insufficient.

Let me finish my previous idea: the gap, as it stands, between the rich world and the poor world is not only morally wrong, but practically infeasible. It is a huge source of global problems. Look at European countries such as France, England, and Germany, where many southern immigrants come seeking employment. Many are Muslims who mainly procure low-level jobs. As they increase in number, local people begin to feel uncomfortable. The basis of the problem is not the Muslims, but the economic gap. If Turkey and the various countries of Africa, from where these people tend to emigrate, were developing properly, their inhabitants would not want to leave. Not only is this situation morally unjust, but by letting the economic gap remain or increase we are creating huge problems for ourselves.

Fabien: Part of the problem is that the money of poorer, "third world" countries has practically no value in terms of global economic standards. Northern countries use southern countries as just a part of their production line.

Dalai Lama: I think the southerners also have an important role to play in finding ways to bridge the gap and making things equal. The main responsibility lies on their shoulders. They should work harder at it. I recently visited Gabon, in Central Africa. I was told the soil is good, but that local people are quite apathetic and that a small, Western-educated elite controls the whole country. Not only is there a large gap between northerners and southerners, but this divide also exists *within* poorer countries: a small, circle of people live like Westerners, while the masses remain scantily dressed and poorly nourished. I find this very sad.

In these circumstances, the money northern countries give to southern countries is wasted. The poor country's elite spends all the funds building skyscrapers with immense halls and air conditioning—which is all very good—but on the outskirts of cities and in rural areas there is nothing—no progress, no development. Surely it would be better if this Western-educated elite were to develop proper motivation, care more for their people, and invest in a truly useful infrastructure. The southern countries must also invest in education. I think education is essential.

In any case, all the natural resource specialists with whom I have spoken warn me that this gap between the "haves" and "have nots" should be reduced. At present, there are 5.5 billion human beings on earth. If the living standard of the southerners were raised to the level the northerners are presently enjoying, what would happen to the world's natural resources? This situation would not be sustainable. China, for example, has a population of 1.2 billion. If each family were to have two cars, the environmental damage would be unimaginable. Nine hundred million people live in India.

The Western concept of increasing the GNP each year must change, and fast. The principle itself contradicts all natural and logical laws.

Fabien: Do you think Westerners should also have fewer cars?

Dalai Lama: Certainly. They need to develop a sense of contentment and more consideration toward others. Things should be done in a more just, equal manner. In the meantime, the birth control question must also be addressed. The southern countries must curb their population growth.

Fabien: Efficient birth control mainly depends on standard of living. The more access to education women have, the fewer children they produce, statistically speaking. So, education seems to be the best way to curb the population explosion.

Dalai Lama: That's very good. But what education? To tell you the truth, I think the first thing the southerners must do is recognize the negative consequences of the present Western concepts of life and economy. We have to correct or remould this erroneous belief in the value of an ever-increasing GNP.

Likewise, although some factories and industries are now adopting new ways to protect the environment, the northerners are inflicting a lot of damage on the world's environment. This prompts me to say that from a global point of view the money produced by the northern world is still insufficient.

Fabien: Do you believe that money has magical power?

Dalai Lama: No! Absolutely not! Yet, people in industrialized nations can no longer survive without money. This explains the critical role money plays in our lives and why people's attitude toward money has changed over time. If you visit Tibetan nomads, you will notice that money means virtually nothing to them. In fact, their animal herds fulfill practically all their daily requirements. This situation is changing now. These nomads have been introduced to thermoses, for example. Now they want to buy thermoses and, at this point, they realize money is necessary to acquire things. For most of us, trade has developed to a point where it can't function without money. Thus it is logical to respect money. There is nothing wrong with that.

Another factor to consider in our attitude toward money is the concomitant lack of spiritual experience that pervades most modern, industrialized life. For example, not necessarily all Tibetans but at least those whose spiritual experience is deeper appreciate money for what it is, while acknowledging that there are other, more essential values. Most people, however, lack this cultivated spiritual experience, and society as a whole abides by the rules of money and power.

Fabien: I would also like to discuss the subject of power with you. In Tibetan I think you say *wangtang—*

Dalai Lama: But first, regarding money, have I made myself clear?

Fabien: It's clear, but I'm a bit disappointed. You said that money is important, that it has its own value, that it is useful, and that it is good to share it.

Dalai Lama: I also said money is not everything. There are other values.

Fabien: Yes, but those who ignore these values think that money is the highest goal. I think that money has stepped beyond the boundaries of its useful, basic functions.

Dalai Lama: Of course, some people are very much involved in money. They can spend almost twenty-four hours a day thinking about it. But the same can be said of a musician or a singer. All their thoughts and energy are spent on music. They even forget to eat and sometimes their health deteriorates. I think this is human nature.

Fabien: But it seems as if the whole structure of our society is based primarily on making money?

Dalai Lama: That is characteristic of industrialized nations. You cannot wear or eat your robots and your machines, so money has become a priority. A farmer can always manage to eat and make clothes with what he cultivates. He can survive without money. In an industrialized nation that is no longer the case. Everything must be bought from a shop. How could one possibly obtain food from a supermarket without money? If I went to a supermarket with a loaf of homemade bread and tried to exchange it for vegetables, it would never work!

Fabien: Not yet.

Dalai Lama: This whole structure did not develop overnight. It took a long time.

Fabien: I agree. Let us come back to the question of power. Where does power come from?

Dalai Lama: Power? It comes from guns!

Fabien: Pardon?!

Dalai Lama: I think that's really true.

Fabien: Okay, then we can go straight to the next subject!

Dalai Lama: There are many different kinds of power. True power comes from serving and helping others. Such behavior makes people respect you. They are willing to listen to your views and advice, and they support you. The energy of many people is thus channeled through one person. This kind of power is positive and authentic. In democratic countries, politicians make many promises so that people will support and respect them. Unfortunately, once they have power, those promises become secondary.

Genuine power exists, but it is difficult to say that one single individual is powerful. Physical power is a primitive concept. It may apply to most animals, but it is no longer apt for human beings. Our concept of power changed when we started giving priority to intelligence. Nowadays power does not stem from a single individual, but comes from the masses, who then entrust this power to an individual whose motivation they believe to be authentic. In the negative sense, a single person can become powerful by threatening the masses with violence. But that power is aggressive and cruel.

Fabien: But there is also a kind of indirect power. Take the example of Mao Tse-tung or Stalin. They did not initially acquire power through violence, but through ideas. Are such people born with power, or is it the result of their karma?

Dalai Lama: It is due to karmic factors, as well as present causes and circumstances.

Fabien: Does that mean those people are more or less responsible than if no karmic factors were involved?

Dalai Lama: There may be a difference in the level of their responsibility, but when we speak of karma, in this instance, it simply means that the person who commits the act reaps the results. In that sense, power is not a blessing bestowed by God. It is also possible that, at the time of birth, a person may not have the karma to be powerful, but that he or she accumulates or creates such karma, thereby changing the course of things within his or her lifetime.

Anne: If power is no longer based on physical strength, but rather on intelligence, does that mean power is the capacity to manipulate others, using aggressive or astute ideas?

Dalai Lama: Cheating—

Anne: Or promising—

Dalai Lama: Yes.

Anne: But can that intelligence also be rooted in *bodhicitta* (altruism)?

Dalai Lama: Yes. There is an essential difference, however, between power acquired through, or dependent on, wrong means, such as guns and cheating, and power that arises from bodhicitta. The former kind of power is short lived. No one respects Mao, Lenin, or Stalin anymore, whereas Mahatma Gandhi is still respected by millions of people.

Fabien: When a person obtains power, by whatever means, and uses it negatively, is the karma created weightier than if he had less power?

Dalai Lama: Of course, if you are talking about the karmic result for that individual.

Fabien: So, that person's responsibility is greater.

Dalai Lama: Yes. As I mentioned earlier, when one person kills another out of desperation, he acquires the sin of killing one person. But a general, who people generally consider a hero, has the power to order his soldiers to kill thousands of people on the battlefield. He will reap the negative result of all the death and suffering that result from his order. Individual soldiers only carry the karmic burden that corresponds to the number of persons they have killed. Responsibility depends more on intention and attitude than on the physical action itself. The general does not physically kill one hundred thousand people, but he makes the decision to allow this killing to occur. Therefore, he is responsible.

Fabien: Unfortunately, when people acquire power, they try to use it for personal goals. In your experience, do politicians also strive for power and forget their responsibility when they achieve it?

Dalai Lama: That depends entirely on the person's motivation and goal. Some people achieve power by being genuinely helpful to others and continue to use that power responsibly, with sincere motivation. That is an example of right action in relation to power.

In the business world, you can become a billionaire through hard work. Other people respect you because you are rich. You can then use that status to make more money, and as long as you make money in an ethical way, it is fine. Your motivation may not be positive, but at least it is not negative. If you adopt questionable methods to become even richer, such as selling arms or building poultry farms, then your livelihood becomes a source of negative energy and karma. By investing your money in the poultry industry, for example, you may become richer, but at the expense of many other beings' lives. There are many investment fields that are ethical or neutral, such as cultivating new plants, developing technology for domestic use, recycling waste material, and so on. Even without positive motivation, at least one does no harm by supporting and benefiting from these activities. Powerful people need to realize the responsibility they hold and be more cautious about their motivation and their acts.

Fabien: Do you think it is acceptable that someone can become a head of state, wielding tremendous responsibility over the lives of many people, without having a "license to power"?

Dalai Lama: In democratic countries, a vote is a license. If a politician proves to be incompetent, he or she will be defeated at the next elections. Another good thing about democracy is the separation of legislative, executive, and judiciary power.

Fabien: Is that sufficient?

Dalai Lama: I don't know, but at least this creates some kind of a protection against power-hungry politicians.

These days I also think the media have an important role to play in this issue of power. When politicians try to do something discretely, journalists come snooping around with their sharp eyes and long noses, like elephants. I like to tease my journalist friends during my press conferences. It is important that journalists also keep a close watch on their own motivations, which should remain sincere.

Fabien: When you meet other heads of state, such as Clinton, Mitterrand, and others, do you try to influence them in subtle ways, with the intention of helping them to act more serenely?

Dalai Lama: Fundamentally I do not distinguish between the people that I meet, whether they are beggars, the pope, or President Clinton—I meet them on the human level. Whether or not I try to engage someone depends on his or her receptivity and attitude. A certain president I met really wanted to exchange ideas with me on a deeper, spiritual level. Of course, I wanted to contribute to his spiritual development in whatever way I could. When I first met with Jacques Chirac, who was mayor of Paris at the time, we discussed compassion and tolerance at length.

Fabien: Considering the huge responsibility these leaders bear, don't you try to instill a small seed of consciousness in them, so that as leaders of human communities they become more awake?

Dalai Lama: Leaders or not, if they are not receptive, I never try to put my ideas in their minds. If a person tends to be a little bit arrogant, I also try to be arrogant. I'm compelled to. If the other person feels something genuine in our meeting, then I also feel something. There is no reason for me to bow my head unnecessarily. Usually, during these meetings, if the other person is somewhat negative, my sentences get shorter and I rely more on my translator. If the other person is sincere, I try to manage in my own broken English.

Let me give you another example. Some thirty years ago I met an Englishman, Felix Green, who was quite a close friend to the late Zhou Enlai of China. Mr. Green had visited China regularly for many years and had great faith in both the country and in communism. He came to Dharamsala with several films, hoping to show me how happy people were in Tibet, and to explain that things were not as bad as we, the Tibetans living in exile, believed. He tried to convince me that everything was okay in my country. We talked and argued for three or four days. After many hours of discussion, he finally changed his attitude on most points. In such cases, a good argument based on sincere motivation can produce a positive result, provided both parties strive to be objective. It is very helpful to talk, talk, talk, until a solution is found.

Fabien: But when you have opportunities for such exchanges with other heads of state, do you take them?

Dalai Lama: That's very difficult. My time with heads of state rarely exceeds half an hour!

Fabien: I was hoping you might use some kind of magical power.

Dalai Lama: If I had magical power, I would have long since used it on Deng Xiao-ping. A complete failure! I have no magical power.

Fabien: Do you think it would be helpful if the world's heads of state meditated for five or ten minutes each day?

Dalai Lama: Definitely. More than thirty years ago in Darjeeling, I participated in a spiritual function with the Karmapa [the head of the *Kagyu* School of Tibetan Buddhism]. The former chief minister of West Bengal gave a speech in which, as a gesture of humility, he stated, "I'm not a spiritual person, I'm a politician." When my turn to speak came, I replied, half-jokingly—but actually quite seriously—that spirituality is far more important for a politician than for someone who remains secluded in the mountains seeking spiritual awakening. A hermit, even if he is not involved in spirituality, will not be able to harm the public, but the same cannot be said for a politician. A politician is an important figure in society and has a great need for spirituality. If such a person's mind becomes crooked, then he or she can be truly harmful to many people. Therefore, it is essential that leaders of nations cultivate peace of mind, an altruistic attitude, and a true sense of universal responsibility.

Fabien: Do you know any leaders apart from you who meditate regularly?

Dalai Lama: That is difficult to say. Actually, one or two of them have asked me for spiritual advice.

Fabien: Do you feel closer to John Lennon, the dreamer, or to Gandhi, the politician?

Dalai Lama: ?!

Fabien: Let me explain. Lennon was not a head of state, but a famous singer. His song "Imagine All the People" was a huge success worldwide. Here, I brought you a copy.

Dalai Lama:

"Imagine there's no heaven, it's easy if you try,
No hell below us, above us only sky.
Imagine all the people, living for today.
Imagine there's no country, it isn't hard to do;
Nothing to kill or die for, and no religion too.
Imagine all the people, living life in peace.
You may say I'm a dreamer, but I'm not the only one.
I hope someday you will join us, and the world will be as one.
Imagine no possessions, I wonder if you can;
No need for greed or hunger, a brotherhood of man.
Imagine all the people, sharing all the world.
You may say I'm a dreamer, but I'm not the only one."

Fabien: Lennon ardently defended world peace. That is one of the reasons he was shot—like Mahatma Gandhi, Martin Luther King Jr., and Anwar Sadat. His ideas were wonderful, but he was not a typical world leader.

Your Holiness, you are the spiritual and temporal leader of the Tibetan people, and today you live in exile. You have the same charisma as Gandhi, but you do not have the influence of someone like Clinton or other world leaders. How do you perceive yourself: as a symbol of hope or something more pragmatic? What is the role of the Fourteenth Dalai Lama in the world peace process?

Dalai Lama: I don't know.

Fabien: Are you a dreamer, an actor, or maybe both?

Dalai Lama: I have a very close connection with Tibet and the

Tibetans, and in that context I usually define myself as a non-violent freedom fighter. So, you see, I'm not really like Lennon. But at the same time, I don't know. This makes me very sad. It is difficult for the Tibetans because my two roles are intertwined. To other people, the Dalai Lama is just another human being who dreams of a peaceful, demilitarized world. A simple Buddhist monk, with neither power nor country. But I can't help it—I feel responsible for all these Tibetan refugees who have such a close connection with their country.

I do not think that world peace is simply a dream, I think we can make it happen. We have to make an effort. World peace is possible!

GLOBAL COMMUNITY

Global Community

Fabien: Your Holiness, some people, including you, say it is important that we create a non-political, economically neutral world organization that would intervene in the fields of ecology, arms, and health. What criteria do you suggest for creating and running such an organization?

Dalai Lama: In fact, I've already reflected on the subject, and my ideas are expounded in a pamphlet called *Global Community and the Need for Universal Responsibility* (see appendix). I definitely think that some sort of new council would be useful. The United Nations, in its present state at least, is an assembly of political representatives of different governments. The top priority of each representative is naturally to defend the interest of his or her government. One may ask to what extent they really represent the people. We need a world body where each member's function is to protect humanity in general, without considering "my nation," "my continent," "my religion," or "my culture" first. The well-being of humanity at large would be their main concern, beyond all notions of artificial frontiers.

The other day I had the idea of forming an international council of sages. Each country would elect representatives who were neither government officials nor politicians. They would choose men and women who were unbiased humanists with a genuine concern for regional, national, and international affairs. These selections would be made at every level—city, region, country, continent. By sages I do not mean religious persons; we need people who are genuinely concerned about ecology, human rights, nuclear power, disarmament, and so on.

Fabien: The UN is already considering disarmament.

Dalai Lama: Hmm.... For the moment, their main focus is arms reduction, and that only applies to nuclear weapons. The UN is just starting to raise the possibility of eliminating nuclear weapons, but no one is talking about general demilitarization. One of my dreams—but it is only a dream—is global demilitarization.

Fabien: How could that work? Cities will always need police.

Dalai Lama: Wherever there are human beings one is bound to find a few mischievous persons. So, when necessary, force may be used. Police forces will still be needed. We will also need some sort of commando unit. But that should be based on a joint, international effort. If such a concept is too vast or premature, one can start on a regional level and create a very efficient collective force to watch over that region of the world, with a few thousand people from each country. Eventually these regional forces would join an international organization. But there should be no more military forces belonging to individual nations.

Fabien: In your dream it seems there are no more nations.

Dalai Lama: That's right. In the real world, French and German troops are already working together. Thanks to this situation, a war between France and Germany is no longer possible. This is the right direction, and we must continue in it.

Fabien: Fifty years ago no one would have ever believed it was possible. It was much more improbable than any dream.

Dalai Lama: That is how we could start. It is not necessary to demilitarize all the nations at once. The forces of individual nations could unite in a single commando unit.

Fabien: To fight whom?

Dalai Lama: Outsiders, of course! [He laughs.] Mind you, if China becomes a superpower without changing its totalitarian system, then Europe and other Western countries must be fully prepared to face it.

Seriously, though, Arab countries, the Middle East, northern Africa and even the whole of Africa could work together. Then central and southern Africa could join them. Even if we cannot completely demilitarize each individual nation for a while yet, at least all these nations could reduce their forces and associate with their neighbors. This would greatly reduce the danger of conflict.

Fabien: Between individual countries perhaps, but it might increase the risk of conflict between larger groups, between Arab and European countries, for example. Regional military units are just one step, not the final goal.

Dalai Lama: Yes, but at least each nation could start demilitarizing. In my vision, the collective forces would be formed from an equal number of people from each country, irrespective of the size of the country or its economy. For example, Luxembourg is a tiny nation, yet it would contribute two thousand people, just like Germany. The commander would be chosen democratically, and this position would rotate between different people at different times. I have already explained such things in some of my texts on global responsibility. I don't think I mentioned joining forces under a single commander, but I clearly expressed the concept of demilitarization.

Fabien: In general are you pessimistic or optimistic?

Dalai Lama: Optimistic.

Fabien: Why?

Dalai Lama: For two reasons. First, I think human nature is basically gentle and compassionate. Second, I am confident that human intelligence, when properly guided, is perfectly capable of finding positive solutions. For me, the twentieth century, with all the experiments and discoveries that have been made, is the most important period in all human history. In the early part of this century, some Marxists and Leninists believed that totalitarian systems would improve humanity. We now know that such theories don't really work. Others thought socialism would be the best answer, but that also seems to have failed.

Personally, I still believe that the idea of socialism is valid. Even Marxism wasn't completely wrong. The recent collapse of the former Soviet Union was not the collapse of Marxism, but of a totalitarian Marxist system. The main defect of the totalitarian system is that it instigates anger and hatred as forces of change. Then again, even as late as the 1970s and 1980s, people thought that ultimate decisions could only be reached through war. That concept has been superseded.

Then came ecology. In the early part of this century, everyone foolishly thought that nature's resources were limitless and at the disposal of humanity. Today ecological ideology even influences political parties. These changes all stem from the experience we have acquired as human beings. In the same way, the concept of human rights, whether individual or general, such as the right to self-determination for a given group, has evolved. These ideas are now universally recognized. Such progress gives me hope for the future.

And of course nuclear weapons are already being reduced. The other day I saw a BBC documentary about the former East Germany. Some people had set up a small, specialized factory where they were producing domestic energy using old bullets and bombs. It seems impossible to dissolve or dismantle these weapons, of which we have huge stocks, but at least we can explode them in a special furnace and recuperate the energy as electricity.

Fabien: It's good to know that human intelligence is capable of transforming deadly machines into something positive.

Dalai Lama: That was really good news, a very positive initiative. So at least nuclear weapons are being reduced. These developments give me hope. However, these are complicated issues. What bothers me is that the more powerful nations that already possess nuclear weapons (and are not willing to give them up) are very pushy about telling other nations that they must not acquire nuclear weapons of their own. That is unjust. Why should the other less powerful nations accept that? I think the five permanent nations of the UN should start by unilaterally disarming *themselves.* They should first get rid of all their nuclear weapons, then they can tell other people not to buy or make such weapons.

Fabien: When I see the fragile balance of power in the world, it looks like children playing games. Egoism and the desire to compete create so much conflict between countries and nations. Where is all this competition leading us?

Dalai Lama: I see two kinds of competition. Our Tibetan tradition trains us, for example, when we say, "I take refuge in the Sangha, the virtuous community," to look up to the community of monks and their discipline as a model of how to live. As such, there is competition, but in a very positive sense. The idea is not to defeat someone, but to do as well or better than they and not lag behind. Sangha has many different levels, ranging from the observance of basic ethics all the way through the ten *bhumi,* or stages, to total enlightenment. The example of such positive, determined beings stimulates us. We can think, "I want to reach that goal, step by step. If others have done it, I also can. At least I will try."

Fabien: In this case, one is competing with oneself, and the fight is against ignorance.

Dalai Lama: Yes. There is competition, but it is used in a good way. It is positive to want to go first, provided the intention is to pave the way for others, make their path more easy, help them, or show the way. Competition is negative when we wish to defeat others, to bring them down in order to lift ourselves up.

Fabien: Don't you sometimes feel world leaders can be very childish in their reactions?

Dalai Lama: Yes, of course. Plenty of people are like that. It happens all the time. I visited the Soviet Union in 1979, at a time when there was a lot of propaganda about how dangerous foreigners were. People stared at me, and I felt weird. I returned years later, when they were less brainwashed, and was pleasantly surprised to find that the Russian people I met on the street were ordinary human beings. For so many years the whole government machine, based on the ideas of one or two individuals, had deliberately created an erroneous impression about the West.

Why not just let people be people? There would be no problem of West and East. We all belong to the same humanity. I often feel that many problems would be solved more easily if they were handled by the people themselves, on a human level. Leaders sometimes make a fuss for nothing. Their intelligence is so sharp that they create all sorts of unnecessary doubts or suspicions. They may not even do it deliberately, but they often complicate the issues rather than simplify them.

I recently discussed an idea that I've been working on for some time. I notice that human beings, through their actions, create a lot of suffering, not only for other human beings, but also for animals. But humans are just one species on this planet, and a recent one at that. Many other species came into existence billions of years ago. All of them, down to the smallest insect, strive to achieve happiness and overcome suffering, as we do. Of course some animals, such as tigers and elephants, make other animals suffer with their power and cunning. But their actions are very limited, and they take another being's life only when they feel hungry, in order to survive. Animals are capable of positive feelings such as compassion, a sense of responsibility, and even tolerance. On the negative side, they get angry and feel hatred and jealousy, just as we do.

In terms of feelings, there is no difference between human beings and other mammals. It is easy to observe feelings in our pets. Dogs and cats have desire, attachment, and even a limited form of altruism. A mother dog will feel a sense of responsibility toward her puppy, and will undergo personal hardship to protect it and care for it. Dogs can also feel hatred, anger, and jealousy. But the destruction that an animal's negative emotions can cause is limited, and their positive emotions are constructive only in their own tiny sphere.

It is human intelligence that makes us so vastly different from other living beings. On the positive side, our intelligence enables us to develop boundless altruism, which is impossible for an animal. There may be a few exceptions, but in general dogs or cats will only continue to feel compassion for a few weeks or months after the object of their compassion is removed from them, whereas human beings who know each other well and cultivate a deep feeling of respect and friendship will maintain this bond until their last day. This capacity stems from our ordinary human intelligence, which can also, when extended, be used to develop bodhicitta, or infinite altruism.

But it is terrifying to see the amount of destruction humans can cause when their intelligence becomes a servant to negative emotions, such as hatred. We have to be wary of this very intelligence, which has caused so much destruction in the world. Although, from a spiritual point of view, we can say that humans are the most precious of all living beings, seen from other angles we are the most destructive species our planet has known. Not only do we create pain for other species—the millions of fish, chickens, cows, and others we consider to be our rightful food—but we use our intelligence even to plan the total destruction of the planet on which we live!

It may seem difficult, but I think it is essential to link economics with compassion. Last year we dismantled several large poultry farms in the Tibetan settlements in South India out of compassion. It happened like this. One day I went to visit a small lake to offer food to the fish that we had previously freed there. On my way back someone said, "By the way, did you see the poultry farm?" All of a sudden I had a vision where I saw large groups of chickens marching along carrying banners on which it was written, "The Dalai Lama not only saves fish, but even feeds them. What does he do for us poor chickens?" I felt terribly sad and sorry for the chickens. The next day I discussed the problem with the relevant officials. "If, for economic reasons, there are no alternatives, then I have nothing to say. But if there is an alternative, please think seriously about dismantling these poultry farms," I said. It seems they agreed, and within a few weeks about eight thousand chickens were released in our Bylakuppe settlement, another one or two thousand in Orissa, and some more in Tenzinkang. We no longer raise poultry in our settlements. I was deeply moved by my people's response and promised to live for at least another twenty years. I said this under the influence of my emotion—it was not a prediction.

Fabien: It seems that our intelligence is the basis of all our perversions, but would you say it is the basis for all our potential, as well?

Dalai Lama: Human intelligence is the source of our problems. But it would be foolish to think that the solution is to reduce intelligence. There is only one way out: we must not let our intelligence be guided by negative and harmful emotions. It must be guided only by proper and positive motivation if it is to become marvelously constructive. Deeply positive emotions such as love and compassion are the most basic components of human nature. That is why it is possible for all human beings to cultivate them.

Fabien: Will you talk a bit about the difference between the Christian notion of compassion and the Buddhist one?

Dalai Lama: Regarding love and compassion—the two are often associated in Tibetan—one should discern various levels. One level is the relationship between a man and a woman, which often implies sexual attraction and a feeling of closeness. Due to the attachment or clinging often associated with this feeling, we tend to classify this type of love as one of conflicted or negative emotions. Another type of love is a mother's compassion, her feeling of closeness toward her nursing baby. A mother doesn't feel passionately attached to her child, nor does she expect anything from it. Yet she is deeply concerned about the child's well-being and is completely committed to doing whatever is best for him or her. That, for me, is real compassion.

Perfect compassion is the love we feel for our enemy. It involves no attachment. We realize this person is an enemy, bent on harming us, so we take every necessary precaution as a countermeasure, while continuing to feel concern and compassion for that person. That is genuine compassion.

Fabien: Does compassion also mean taking on others' suffering, as if it were your own?

Dalai Lama: It does, but let's remain focused on compassion in a general sense for a moment. I want to explain why I believe that a human being's basic nature is compassion. When, as a result of a proper marriage, genuine love and compassion are present in the very first moment of a being's life, the right kind of conception takes place. Otherwise, the result is an unwanted child. There are many unwanted children and abortions because people have sexual relations without any sense of responsibility. Genuine marriage is not only a question of love or sexual desire, but also includes a sense of responsibility, mutual respect, and commitment. When these conditions are met, chances are the parents will take proper care of their child. This, for me, is close to genuine compassion. One does not look on his or her partner with pity, but with respect, closeness, and a sense of responsibility.

From the time of conception and through the entire pregnancy, the mother should be calm and happy. When the mother is peaceful, the child can develop properly. It is very harmful for the fetus when the mother is anxious, fearful, or constantly angry. For the first few weeks after the birth, the main preoccupation for mother and child is nursing. The child is not really aware of who is who, but when nursing, he or she trusts and completely relies on the mother. The mother in turn is filled with a genuine sense of responsibility and tenderness, both of which help the milk flow smoothly. If, during that period, the mother develops feelings of anger or hatred toward the child, her milk may not flow properly. Without milk, a child cannot survive. This proves that our survival in the first days and weeks of life depends entirely on love and compassion.

I like to consider milk the symbol of human affection. We were able to survive, develop, and grow up because of it. However, a child needs more than food to stay alive. Scientists are now recognizing how essential physical contact is to a new-born child. Whether it be a parent's or someone else's, touch is crucial for the development of a child's brain. Even in an otherwise comfortable environment, without direct human contact a baby will not develop harmoniously. Tender contact is essential. Our body needs and appreciates the affection of others.

It is now recognized that children who live in an affectionate family environment are healthier and do better in their studies than children who do not. The sad thing is that people who lack human affection early on find it exceedingly difficult to show love and affection to others later in life. They are often cold or insensitive. One can tell from simple observation that when our mind is at peace, the different elements of the body function in harmony, but when we are constantly angry or frightened, they do not.

We now have scientific proof for what I have always believed: the true foundations of human nature are gentleness and compassion. Our first real teacher of compassion is our mother, or the person who acted as a mother to us—even more than our *lama*, or spiritual teacher. The lama comes later.

Fabien: Sometimes never.

Dalai Lama: And sometimes the lama creates problems! But a mother never creates that kind of problem. Mothers are so positive, so kind. Of course, there are exceptional cases when the mother doesn't care about her child, or dies when her child is an infant. In those cases, someone else can act as the mother. The fact is, if no one had really cared for us in early life, we could not have survived.

Fabien: Do you really think that compassion alone can make the whole world better?

Dalai Lama: Definitely. Let me tell you what is wrong with the world. Look at children. Of course they may quarrel, but generally speaking they do not harbor ill feelings as much or as long as adults do. Most adults have the advantage of education over children, but what is the use of an education if they show a big smile while hiding negative feelings deep inside? Children don't usually act in such a manner. If they feel angry with someone, they express it, and then it is finished. They can still play with that person the following day. For me, that is the honest, natural way for basic human nature to act in such situations.

It seems that education...well, we can't actually blame modern, Western education, because things started to change several centuries ago. When lay schools and academic institutions first became widespread, the Christian Church was still very powerful and respected in society. It taught people to develop a good heart and ethics, while the intellect was addressed by lay institutions. As time passed, these two organizations drifted further and further apart. The Church's influence on society gradually declined. As a result, nobody took care to encourage people to develop a kind heart. Family life became less harmonious, more and more couples divorced. Nobody nurtured a good heart. During this time, the education system gave priority to certain specific forms of intelligence and continued to flourish. Spiritual or ethical training ceased to accompany the development of intelligence, while hatred and negative emotions remained just as powerful an influence as before.

Fabien: Many people feel this lack of balance between their intelligence and their feelings. They feel at a loss and would like to rediscover simplicity in their lives. That's fine, but this basic uneasiness seems to come from not having learned how to cultivate calm and happiness. We have no idea how to slow down or interrupt the flow of our thoughts. We don't even know how to breathe properly. All that is missing in our educational systems.

Dalai Lama: What is missing is ethics, free from any religious connotation. With the help of science—particularly the medical sciences—I think we can develop a code of simple ethics, founded on the basic, positive qualities required by human beings in ordinary secular life.

Fabien: A moral code without any religious concepts?

Dalai Lama: Yes. Religion is useful for those who recognize its value and wish to progress on a spiritual path. But human beings can survive and manage without religion.

Anne: On what principles can science base its ethical theories?

Dalai Lama: On love, not harming others, and respecting all beings. Even animals have these elements in their behavioral patterns. We should start by observing how animals act. They are honest and appreciate it when we are honest with them. If you present something nice to an animal in one hand, while hiding a rope in the other, the creature will know your intention. Yet animals have no religion, no constitution. Basic nature has endowed them with the faculty of discernment. It is the same for humans.

Anne: Your Holiness, how do you want us to trust scientists? After World War II, for example, many Western doctors told mothers it was harmful to breast-feed their babies. Even today, many women don't want to breast-feed. In fact, women are still warned against breast-feeding in some Western hospitals.

Dalai Lama: Yes, but I think new scientific concepts are emerging. Now doctors are saying that breast-feeding reduces a woman's chances of contracting breast cancer.

Anne: Your point is well taken. I'm just afraid it might take a long time for things to change. In the meantime, two generations of Western children have been deprived of this close contact, and the world is in chaos.

Dalai Lama: To create a better, happier world, we must adopt a twofold strategy. First, we must forget about the present generation. It is already contaminated. Instead, we should focus our energies on the younger generation. Second, we must start acting immediately to drastically reduce pollution levels. There are groups of people working in various parts of the world to improve human rights, children's rights, recycling systems, etc. All these things are happening. Some dubious people with little real spiritual training call themselves teachers, but actually take advantage of others in the name of taking care of peace of mind. This is unfortunate. It happens because, when it comes to spirituality, people are still very gullible.

In 1973, during my first trip to Europe, I was invited to a dinner at the home of the late UN refugee commissioner in Geneva. Several important guests were present, but we were talking quite casually. I expressed my feeling that the present generation was quite hopeless. My host was a little shocked. Yet I honestly believe that our first priority should be to prepare a long-term strategy for improving the state of the world that focuses on the coming generations.

Fabien: Do you think that one individual can change the world?

Dalai Lama: Yes.

Fabien: In that case, the best thing to do is to start trying to improve oneself.

Dalai Lama: It seems quite simple. First, it is important to realize we are part of nature. Ultimately, nature will always be more powerful than human beings, even with all their nuclear weapons, scientific equipment, and knowledge. If the sun disappears or the earth's temperature changes by a few degrees, then we are really in trouble.

At a deeper level, we should recognize that although we are part of nature, we can control and change things, to some extent, due to our intelligence. Among the thousands of species of mammal on earth, we humans have the greatest capacity to alter nature. As such, we have a twofold responsibility. Morally, as beings of higher intelligence, we must care for this world. The other inhabitants of the planet—insects and so on—do not have the means to save or protect the world. Our other responsibility is to undo the serious environmental degradation that is the result of incorrect human behavior. We have recklessly polluted the world with chemicals and nuclear waste, selfishly consuming many of its resources. Humanity must take the initiative to repair and protect the world.

Of course, when we say, "humanity" or "society," it's obvious the initiative must come from individuals. A community is simply a collective of individuals. It is wrong to expect our governments, or even God, to give us any guidance on these matters.

Fabien: The Jewish tradition says that that which is above is the same as that which is below. It may be a way of saying that the microcosm and macrocosm are interdependent and by changing one individual—

Dalai Lama: Yes, they are related. This means that *each* individual has the responsibility to change. Changes in the state of the world depend on individual behavior.

Fabien: But can one honestly say to people that if they develop more compassion in their home and work, if they are careful about pollution and more open to what is happening around them, they can change the world? The task seems too huge to most people.

Dalai Lama: True. We have a big problem, and individual effort does seem insignificant. However, this was also the case in the past. For Buddhists, the coming of Buddha Shakyamuni to India and his teachings on the Four Noble Truths and altruism were immensely important, yet no one knew about it outside India. The whole world was not changed. Jesus Christ started teaching in the Middle East, but in the East Indies no one had any notion of Christianity until much later. When one great master appears from time to time on this planet— which is already rare in itself—then there is some change. It's not a complete change, but it is a shift in the right direction.

That was the situation in the past. Nowadays much has changed. People are more aware of both local and global situations and their consequences. If we think properly, there is great hope for improving the present situation. If, through mass media and education, we all become more aware and make a unified, positive effort, our chances of changing humanity's way of thinking is greater than ever before.

You will note here that I'm speaking in terms of humanity. I'm not referring to any particular ideology. If we speak in terms of Buddhist, Christian, or any other ideology, we limit our scope. Let's speak from the perspective of humanity in general, even when we explain the importance of compassion. Let's refer to day-to-day life, not to scriptures. I'm sure general awareness can grow with this perspective.

Fabien: Do you believe in evolution or revolution?

Dalai Lama: Evolution.

Fabien: Does evolution always take a long time, or can it occur suddenly, triggered by some incredible event—of a cosmic nature, perhaps?

Dalai Lama: Compared to the whole of human history, this century has brought many very sudden changes. A century is short—just three generations. Now people everywhere are more aware that something is definitely wrong with our present way of life. They realize that the system does not function properly. More and more people, be they Japanese, Indian, American, Russian, or whatever are concluding that something is missing. This awareness is not a result of God's blessing. It stems directly from our experiences in this century.

Generally speaking, this awareness is more widespread in industrialized and economically developed nations, because those populations have realized that mental frustration is still rampant, despite "development." In countries like India most people still have not overcome basic poverty. What does ecology mean to them? When their survival depends on the firewood they collect, how can you tell people in rural areas not to cut down their forests? How can you tell beggars who sleep in the streets of urban slums not to urinate anywhere? How can you discuss hygiene with the homeless and destitute?

People first have to reach a certain stage of mental evolution. Once their basic needs are met, then they begin to realize, through their own experience, that material comforts are not sufficient to create happiness. People must realize that even with all these comforts, all this money, and a GNP that increases every year, they are still not happy. They need to understand that the real culprits are our unceasing desires. Our wants have no end.

ECONOMICS AND
ALTRUISM

Economics and Altruism

Fabien: Your Holiness, I was intrigued by what you had to say about Marxism at the Congress on Business and Ethics in Paris in 1994. Can you reiterate the distinction you made between original Marxism and what people think it to be?

Dalai Lama: The essential Marxist question is: how is money to be distributed throughout society? While Marxism is based on ethical considerations, the economic theories whose main aim is profit are not. But in practice, Marxism insisted too heavily on hatred toward the rich. Marx's idea of helping the working classes was good; but his system of thought was undermined by its lack of compassion. This shows that material and spiritual considerations must be joined.

Fabien: So, you propose that altruism, as opposed to sheer competition and the desire for money, should be one of the main forces in the business world? This seems very idealistic and far removed from business as most people see it.

Dalai Lama: Finding a way to connect economics and altruism is most difficult. However, these two fields can—and should—meet on global and individual levels.

On the global level, we must take immediate measures to create ethical codes in the worlds of business and finance. Otherwise these two clubs will continue to protect their own interests, while creating extremely serious ecological problems for the rest of the world. We must also remember that economics is responsible for creating the unacceptable gap that exists between nations, and even people of the same nation. If we continue along this path, the situation could become irreparable. The yawning gap between the "haves" and "have nots" is going to create a lot of suffering for everyone, including the world of finance itself. Therefore, let us widen our perspective to include the whole world's well-being and the future generations in our vision of economics.

It is obvious that economics needs to become more humanized. All those who have a role to play in finance and business should develop a sense of responsibility based on altruism and consider what is good for the entire world. Otherwise—and probably sooner than later—the world economies will find themselves in extremely difficult predicaments.

In the early part of this century things were okay, but now we must think carefully about the future, since the human population has greatly increased. The entire world is much more interconnected at present, what you call "globalization." Due to commercial exchanges, currency—which is nothing more than small pieces of paper—has become so important, as we said earlier on. Why? Because without it we cannot function in daily life. We have become too fragile. For me, the indication that something is really wrong with today's world is that when the United States' economy sneezes, the whole world catches a cold.

We should not forget our true goals. Let me give you an example based on my home, here in Dharamsala. If I thought money was of prime importance in obtaining happiness, I could fell all the trees in my garden and thus raise a few thousand rupees. Yet, through this act, I would ultimately create suffering for myself. If all the trees here were cut down, then I would need to sell my tables for money. Finally, I would bring disaster on myself. In reality, making a profit from these material things would have completely defeated my original purpose: the pursuit of happiness. In the same way, one-sided, narrow-minded economies soon deplete all our natural resources. Our land becomes polluted, our water contaminated.

But, in the world of economics, who cares about the earth? What is water to self-centered economists and business people? Their greed and short-sightedness is causing our atmosphere to change, making us all suffer. Such are the negative consequences of the blind pursuit of wealth.

The problem is the same with science. Consider the work of geneticists. Their work appears marvelous, but they only see, study, and manipulate a particular gene, often missing the wider consequences of their actions. Many of the physicists who created the various forms of atomic and nuclear energy may not have intended to make atom bombs and destroy so many innocent lives, but this was nevertheless the consequence of their inventions. Catastrophes like dropping the atom bomb will result from narrow economic views. We are repeating the same errors. Is that clear now?

Fabien: Yes, it is quite frightening. That is the global level.

Dalai Lama: Yes. Now for the individual level. The very purpose of making money is to satisfy one's needs. Sometimes it is just for the relief of being able to say, "I have plenty of money." It's true—poor people are always full of anxiety. One would think that once people have lots of money, they would be content with their wealth. However, millionaires often want more and more wealth. They never achieve genuine satisfaction. I have friends in the business world. Some are rich and I often tease them, half-jokingly, "So now you are liberated from poverty, but you have become a slave to money. The fact is, you are never satisfied."

Fabien: Kalu Rinpoche once said, "A person who has no money is always thinking about money. A person who has too much money is always thinking about money. Neither has any peace of mind." Rich people not only work to earn money, but also struggle to keep what they have. They are always afraid of losing their wealth.

Dalai Lama: So, the result is the opposite of their original intention. They have lost sight of their purpose. They wanted to make money to become free and satisfied, but when they have money they feel no mental satisfaction, not to mention contentment. They are neither happy nor satisfied. What is the use?

Fabien: Let us look at money from another angle. Money, like power, seems to have a perverse effect on most people's mind. Except to present an economic theory or organize a colloquium, who would dare mention ethics in the world of business and finance? The business world stands apart from humanity, as if it were some country with its own separate legal system. How will it ever be possible to introduce notions of kindness and altruism into such a milieu?

Dalai Lama: Altruism has two aspects. Loving others does not mean that we should forget ourselves. When I say we should be compassionate, this does not mean helping others at the expense of ourselves. Not at all. Sometimes I say the buddhas and bodhisattvas are the most selfish of all. Why? Because by cultivating altruism they achieve ultimate happiness. We, in our selfishness, are very foolish and narrow-minded. All we do is create more suffering for ourselves. The selfishness of the buddhas and bodhisattvas is functional and efficient. It allows them to achieve not only awakening, but also the capacity to help others. That is really worthwhile. For me, this proves that to create maximum happiness for oneself, one needs to develop compassion. This is Buddhist logic. If compassion induced misery, then it would be questionable. Why practice something that brings us more trouble? But that is certainly not the case with compassion. Just imagine if we all lived with no compassion, thinking only of ourselves. We would suffer greatly. The more you think of others, the happier you are.

Fabien: I was so shocked when, in Berlin, you said something like, "Be selfish. Think about others." So, altruism is intelligent selfishness?

Dalai Lama: That's right. But let us return to economics. When we say that we need compassion and altruism in the business world, it means that people working in the areas of commerce and finance should become more aware of the wider negative or positive consequences of their decisions and activities. When general negativity occurs, ultimately we will all suffer.

I cherish myself and do not want to suffer. The problem is, if I put all my energy into creating personal happiness, eventually I will reap pain and suffering as a result of my neglect of others. Yet if I embrace altruism, I naturally develop not only a greater sense of love and responsibility, but also a wider perspective. That is the main point.

Fabien: Let's say you are running a company, and you make an effort to be open-minded—at least until you learn to be truly altruistic—and donate a certain share of your profits to people in need. But you also have to take into account the money the government takes from you and what it does with it, like spend it on defense.

Dalai Lama: Arms?

Fabien: Yes. You are surely aware that while some of our governments' activities are altruistic, many are directed solely toward making profits, or creating weapons, sometimes of mass destruction. Huge amounts of money we have earned are swallowed up without any wisdom and we have nothing to say about it. It is so frustrating. I see no way to change the direction of these government machines that continue to crush people as they blunder on toward disaster.

Dalai Lama: You see, I told you this generation is lost, polluted. The whole system you have established has created this situation. To argue about these things, I think we have to go deeper into human nature. For example, I think we can say that human beings—whether educated or uneducated—react very strongly against the idea of neutron bombs. Why? I think neutron bombs are marvelous. They are surely one of the greatest human achievements, because they are designed to reach their target unfailingly. Their target is just human beings, not houses, not buildings. Everything inorganic is left untouched. Only living beings— plants, too—die. But the good thing is that the enemy, the one we are trying to get at, is undoubtedly destroyed.

Who is our enemy? The human being. That is the real troublemaker. In usual warfare, not only does the opposing army suffer, but whole cities are also destroyed, and many innocent people in present and future generations suffer as well. The neutron bomb is very clean and honest. The real troublemakers are eliminated, but no damage is done to the buildings. So, when the war is finished, new people can just move in, comfortably.

Anyhow, the point is that not only are powerful people like politicians, technicians, and military chiefs against this bomb—*everyone* is against it. They are terrifying to human beings. The true horror of negative intelligence appears very nakedly. We have created a super powerful weapon, a mass killer exposed in all its technological splendor. That is what I'm getting at. People naturally sense there is something terrible about such an invention. It has nothing to do with religion. It is basic human awareness.

That reminds me of another observation I've made. I'm going to test it on you, Fabien. If I set a glass of blood and a glass of milk before you on this table, which would you prefer?

Fabien: I would prefer the milk. I don't like the sight of blood.

Dalai Lama: Why?

Fabien: Because blood means suffering. When you cut yourself or you are injured, you bleed.

Dalai Lama: Yes. But without blood we cannot survive. The brain, especially, needs blood, not milk. So, in fact, blood is more important to us. We occasionally need milk, but we always need blood. When someone is gravely hurt, one speaks of blood transfusions, not milk transfusions. Blood sustains life. In truth, we should feel more close to blood than to milk. But we also feel, as you rightly mentioned, that blood means pain, that our body is injured when we bleed. Bleeding usually happens as a result of fighting, anger, or hatred, so when we see blood, we feel frightened. Milk is a result of love and compassion, so when we see milk, we feel peace.

Although, in a sense, blood is more fundamental to us than milk, the fact that we perceive blood as a result of suffering and milk as a product of peace proves that in some innate way we are attracted to peace, love, and compassion, whereas we feel repulsion for violence and blood.

Human nature is profoundly sensible. I propose that all our activities, especially economics and warfare, be conducted according to a more natural, human approach. Nowadays we are quite unaware of our true human nature—our intelligence is so powerful that it clouds this innate, compassionate, and organic disposition.

Fabien: So you think that we have alienated ourselves from our genuine human nature?

Dalai Lama: I think so. When we think about neutron bombs and other such things, our instinctive nature reacts. As far as economics is concerned, however, we have a twofold dilemma: the potential dangers of non-altruistic economics are not immediately perceptible, and our short-sighted desires tend to overwhelm the messages of basic human nature. But at least our basic humanity still revolts against the most horrifying things, thank goodness.

Fabien: Everything you say is so logical and sensible. Could you advise us as to how, in a very simple way, we could rediscover our basic humanity?

Dalai Lama: Advice? If I were a dictator, I would—[He bursts into laughter]. If I had all the power in the world, I would set up a proper plan for the long-term future, based on education that is in tune with human nature, a system that would allow basic human qualities to blossom to their fullest possible extent. Then, regarding the present situation—hee, hee!—I would lock up all the people who have no concern for their basic human value in a concentration camp. And the first one I would lock up would be *you*, Fabien! That would be mutually beneficial: first there would be less trouble in society, and second you would lose weight!

Okay, let's be serious. It is very difficult for me to give advice. It is the media and the writers who must warn people about the disasters we will have to face if the present social, economic, and spiritual situations continue along their present trajectories.

Actually, I'm quite optimistic. Take the example of environmental problems. The scientists and associations that defend the environment have repeatedly informed us about the ecological problems now facing the earth, like global warming and widespread pollution of our water and air. Now, awareness is growing worldwide. New techniques are evolving so that we can avoid pollution without changing the process of industry or the economy. During a recent visit to Stockholm, my friends told me that ten years before the fish had practically disappeared from the nearby river. Now they are regenerating, simply because the industrial plants along that river have made some effort to protect the environment. In other words, they managed to improve the situation without destroying the industry. I was recently in the Rohr region of Germany, a center of industry. One large company showed me a film on the different means they were taking to reduce pollution and recycle waste material. Without changing their entire structure, they were causing much less damage to the environment. This is the way.

Concern for ecology grows with the proper and widespread dissemination of information. People have gradually become convinced that the situation is serious and that we must take care of our planet. I've noticed that now, in some hotels, we are asked not to waste electricity or water. This is a good start. Likewise, the media must speak of the importance of altruism in every human activity. It must be discussed again and again, in newspapers, in the movies, on the radio, on TV. I think there is plenty of momentum to do this. Medical and scientific fields should support the theory of altruism. Ecologists will support it, as will the peace movement. Logically, each family will encourage the movement, providing the educational system is also improved so that children become less violent. Then, even the police force will change, and everyone will gradually begin to think and act with more kindness, altruism, and compassion.

Some time ago, I was speaking with a Swiss friend who works for a non-governmental organization that teaches ethics and peace. At first, local education authorities were suspicious of, and reluctant to work with, his organization. Eventually, the Swiss government approached my friend, saying, "We have noticed your methods are effective in preventing violence in the schools. We would like you to participate more in the schools." This is just one example. I think it will eventually be possible for governments to lay down a policy that supports this idea of basic humanity and altruistic activity. The UN could follow.

Fabien: Your Holiness, as individuals, we can choose to invest our savings in those sectors of the economy that are positive, rather than support arms factories or the chemical industry. Will this accelerate change toward a better world? Is it an efficient way of putting pressure on destructive sectors of our society?

Dalai Lama: Generally speaking, I think there is nothing wrong with chemicals.

Fabien: It depends on what these companies produce and whether their main motivation is profit or the well-being of humanity.

Dalai Lama: We had a rule in Tibet that anyone proposing a new invention had to guarantee that it was beneficial, or at least harmless, for seven generations of humans before it could be adopted.

Fabien: That is a very sensible principle. It has been quite easy to invest funds and get high returns in countries where basic human rights are not respected, like South Africa under apartheid or China at present. What karmic weight do we accumulate by supporting these regimes, even indirectly?

Dalai Lama: Let us not talk of karma, but simply of our responsibility toward the whole world. One should not invest one's money in arms, especially as our goal is to demilitarize on a global level and reduce the arms trade. This kind of passive resistance is a small but definite contribution toward peace. However, such a change requires proper planning and coordination. I recently saw an encouraging example in the former Soviet Union and former East Germany. An arms factory had been adapted so that it could transform heavy military equipment into bull dozers for agricultural purposes. The factory was the same, the product was virtually the same, but the attitude and application shifted.

Fabien: Do you think the need to work is also a basic part of human nature? What if work were not absolutely essential in defining a successful human being?

Dalai Lama: I think your Western way of living and thinking have created your present society, where unemployed persons are considered worthless. I'm under the impression that an unemployed Tibetan would not be so anxious as an unemployed person from the West. Providing he or she had enough to eat and a shelter, life would be great. Such a person might be happy lying around all day, gossiping with friends from time to time!

This is a question of mentality. Actually, in the early fifties my good friends the Chinese communists gave me some lessons on this topic. When I visited Mao Tse-tung in Beijing in 1954, he explained that the goal of communism was total freedom. Of course, to begin with, we had to work during the week. That way we would appreciate the week-end holiday. As development progressed, the situation would invert. There would be less work and more free time, more entertainment. In fact, everyone would have so little work that any short period of labor would become a holiday! No class distinction. Work for everyone. Take what you need. There would be no "mine" and "yours."

Although the present unemployment situation in industrialized countries seems very unpleasant, I feel that the concepts your society created are to blame. The main culprit is this very perverse idea that profits have to increase every year. Your economists warn you that unless the GNP increases every year, the country is headed for disaster. From this perspective, unemployed people are seen as unproductive— an ominous sign of regression.

Fabien: It is a problem of never being satisfied.

Dalai Lama: Right. If the generally accepted concept was to obtain what we really need and then be content, society would be completely different. We would not always be tortured by that kind of fear and anxiety. We could just relax and be happy. Developing a sense of contentment is a precious gift. Unemployment would not seem so negative. Then, we could use our free time in a positive way.

Fabien: Very often, unemployed persons feel guilty.

Dalai Lama: One always feels guilty when one lives on another's work. Sharing work seems to be a good idea. For example, a factory with one hundred employees could take on another hundred employees half-time with half-salary. The first team could work one week and rest the following week, when the second team could work. Then everyone would have a job and feel useful.

Fabien: That brings us back to the question of altruism. Most people are ready to share the work, but not the money.

Dalai Lama: It would probably not cost more than unemployment.

Anne: As he grew older, my father's vision was that, by nature, man was not made to work. His proposal was that from birth until death each human being was entitled to have his basic needs met: food, shelter, clothes, education. Those who wanted to earn more and become rich could do so, but there would be two monetary systems: virtual money, which would allow everyone to live decently, and hard money for those who wanted to be rich.

Dalai Lama: It's true that a double system might work. At one time people were very much attracted to socialism. The kibbutz in Israel was a great example. The spirit of the kibbutz is declining now, but the original idea of the first generation was really wonderful. Within one country, people could choose their way of life according to their own beliefs. Not all Israelis lived in the kibbutz, but those who believed in this system were free to live this lifestyle, with an independent system of economic production.

In this way, it would be possible to have socialist, communist, or capitalist communities living harmoniously within one nation, without interfering with one another. Later, when national boundaries disappear, there will no longer be any reason to base things on *my* culture, or *my* system. Each nation would become multicultural and embrace all spiritual traditions. Each economy also would be a multifaceted system. National boundaries would lose their meaning.

The unemployed could also create a community where everybody could sleep late, then gossip for a few hours, have some entertainment, and take some exercise. The members of the community at large wouldn't need to feel jealous of them. There would be no need for competition. Those who want to lead that kind of life should be able to do so.

Anne: I'm not sure how often people "choose" unemployment. It is generally imposed on them.

Dalai Lama: Hmm…. I have no answer now. National boundaries really create a lot of these problems. Industrialized nations, in general, have plenty of money and technology. Instead of sending out their military missions to "help" underdeveloped countries—Africa, for example—why don't they really help them make their deserts fertile and improve their living conditions? How many square miles of desert did the Israelis turn into green valleys? We have the capacity to change things, if we want to.

I suggest this as a long-term plan under a world government. As we discussed the other day, once we have a council of sages, the world can be demilitarized. Once major sources of fear are removed, then we can start working on the question of economic power. The main point is that all decisions should be taken within the perspective of global responsibility.

Fabien: Your Holiness, I would like to talk with you about religion. Does society need religion? Is it an individual need, or is it a necessary foundation for politics, and for greater human communities? Can we function without religion?

Dalai Lama: Religion is a question of individual freedom. Basically, I cannot say that humanity needs religion because observation proves that we can survive perfectly well without it. In fact, a great majority of the 5.7 billion humans on this planet are non-believers. Still, I do think that religion has an important role in human societies. But I normally make a distinction between religion and spirituality. Spirituality has two levels: internal and external. The external level is simply to remain a kind, warm-hearted human being who does not harm others, who is law abiding, and does not lie or kill, as we mentioned earlier. We can do that without belonging to any religion.

Inner spirituality helps develop and strengthen our intrinsic qualities, and in this sense I think that religion has an important role to play, since it gives hope to some individuals. In this way, the major religious traditions have great potential. It is wrong to assume that all human requirements can be fulfilled by external means, without using our inner qualities. As human beings, a positive core is essential for survival. Religions can help with this.

However, I don't agree when some religions say that it is impossible to develop these deeper human qualities without the grace of God. This is a problem. If I were to say that these positive human qualities only arise or increase from the grace or the blessings of the Buddha, then I would be implying that non-Buddhists are denied that opportunity. It is not right to say that a person who doesn't believe in God cannot improve.

Fabien: That is the danger of "organized" religion. Heads of religious orders often try to keep "their" people under control by instilling fear or guilt in them.

Dalai Lama: Yes, I've heard of the notion of a "God-fearing people." This only confirms me in the path I am trying to follow. I will definitely contribute whatever I can to humanity from my tradition and experience, but I give no importance at all to "propagating the Dharma."

Fabien: Do you ever get accused of proselytizing? After all, you are a religious teacher.

Dalai Lama: No, it's not a problem. Basically, I recognize the wide variety of mental dispositions among human beings. This is totally acceptable to me. The Buddha himself clearly acknowledged that some of his followers believed in the bodhisattva's path and others did not. He knew that the *Mahayana* path of the bodhisattva was deeper and better, yet to those who could not follow it he said, "Your own nirvana is the ultimate goal." It is for those Buddhists who were not prepared for full buddhahood that the *sutras* mention three ultimate goals: two lower states of *arhatship* and buddhahood. The Buddha said this recognizing different people's different circumstances and capacities. This is why there are four schools of Buddhist thought with many contradictions between them. The Buddha created all these schools to accommodate the different mental dispositions of his followers. If in Buddhism alone so many dispositions exist, then there must be many more in the human family. Buddhism alone cannot fulfill all these different needs.

My basic feeling is that it is better for people to follow their own religious tradition. This is the message I give to Christian countries. Buddhists like you should think very carefully. Maybe you realize that the Buddhist way is really more effective, but you must be absolutely certain this approach is for you. If you are sure, then you have the individual right to change. If you waiver at all, it is better to follow your own tradition.

Fabien: One hears strange things these days, like the story of American Protestants who signed up at the University of Lhasa, Tibet, so that they could stay in Tibet and convert the Tibetans, or the story of zealous missionaries in Mongolia. I heard that one smart Mongolian managed to earn thirty dollars by getting baptized three times. Yesterday I read about a group of people of Hindu origin who want to renounce their conversion to Christianity, declaring they became Christians in exchange for help when they were in dire need. What do you think of missionaries?

Dalai Lama: Missionary zeal stems from religious leadership and policy, but it also often arises from sincere desire. In the early 1960s, many Tibetan refugees were working in labor camps in Kulu, India, making roads in the mountains. One day, I met an American lady who told me, "These Tibetans are so sweet. Even under exceedingly difficult conditions, they are cheerful and smiling. They sing all day long, but I feel so sorry for them." She started to cry. "Such nice people, but they have no religion." She had not only missed that their songs were prayers, but she could not see beyond "One God, One Truth." She was very sincere, but she had no knowledge of other religions.

Fabien: I don't have this problem, because I was born amongst the "chosen people"!

Dalai Lama: So, you are a liberal Jew. I have had several dialogues with some prominent Jewish scholars and mystics. They really appreciated our discussions. Once, a Jewish scholar voiced his concern about the fact that some of the most brilliant Jews had converted to Buddhism. I told him that I never attempt to convert anyone. In the Buddhist tradition, you never ask someone to change their religion. This would be considered a lack of respect for others. On the other hand, if people approach us, seeking teachings, it is our responsibility to answer their requests.

As I mentioned before, I believe that it is better for people to follow their own tradition. I understood this man's concern. The Jewish community is small, and if some of its best scholars are attracted to Buddhism, it may cause a practical problem. Previously, different religious communities were more isolated. As long as Buddhists remained in their countries, Muslims in theirs, and Christians in theirs, it didn't matter if they had one religion or a specific concept of God. Today the situation is very different. Now, if I try to propagate Buddhism while other religious leaders try to spread Catholicism or Islam, sooner or later there will be a clash. This is the danger.

Religion is important for humanity, but it should evolve with humanity. The first priority is to establish and develop the principle of pluralism in all religious traditions. If we, the religious leaders, cultivate a sincere pluralistic attitude, then everything will be more simple. It is good that most religious leaders are at least beginning to recognize other traditions, even though they may not approve of them. The next step is to accept that the idea of propagating religion is outdated. It no longer suits the times.

Fabien: While we are discussing religion, I would like to ask a few questions about morality within the Buddhist community. What would happen if a monk or a lama committed a serious crime, such as taking money from a disciple or committing a rape? Buddhism is a peaceful religion. Does that mean that discipline is stricter or looser than in other religions?

Dalai Lama: In order to answer this question, I must make a clear distinction between the notion of lama or *guru,* which means spiritual teacher, and that of *tulku,* a reincarnate being who is recognized as such by a Tibetan Buddhist school or a particular lineage of teachers. These are two different things. Recognition as a tulku has gradually come to confer a kind of social status. As a result, people can have a big name without having deep spiritual realization. Sometimes they behave very badly and manipulate people in the name of guru yoga, or other spiritual practices. Blind devotion is dangerous. According to Buddhist teaching, you only come to accept everything the lama does as positive at a very realized level of practice, when both the teacher and the student are well aware of what they are doing. An example of this kind of teacher-disciple relationship at its best is that between Tilopa and Naropa, two of Tibet's most acclaimed masters.

Nowadays, however, there are too many Buddhist "teachers." Some—as long as they lived in the Tibetan community—were never considered masters; but after living abroad for a few years, they returned surrounded by many disciples. I think some people from my government are a bit jealous of their success! Unfortunately, the situations you mention have arisen. For the moment, we have no system to distinguish "recognized" tulkus, for instance, from qualified spiritual teachers.

Fabien: Do you plan to establish one?

Dalai Lama: The issue was raised during a meeting I had with Western Dharma teachers, and many people reacted very strongly, questioning the way in which it could be done. The result was a lot of misunderstanding and sectarianism. It was a simple gathering of teachers, yet some people even accused me of being manipulative and sectarian.

Anne: Forgive me if I'm too frank, but if, in a Tibetan monastery, a young monk had been manipulated or sexually abused by an older monk, would the novice have the courage to speak out? Would anyone listen? If so, what would the sanction be?

Dalai Lama: The sanction would be determined by the religious authority of that monastery. Last year we had one such case, and the senior monk was dismissed from the monastery. In our tradition, novice monks, as well as fully ordained monks, take vows of chastity. They are not allowed to lose their semen, including by means of their own hand. Fully ordained monks have about 253 vows to keep. Chastity is the thirteenth vow, but it is also one of the four cardinal vows, namely: not to kill a human being that is already born or in formation, not to steal, to observe chastity, and not to pretend to have spiritual realizations or capacities that one doesn't have. If broken, these vows cannot be repaired. If you breach the vow of chastity in any way, you are no longer a monk.

According to the rules of discipline, whether someone hears, sees, or suspects a breach of the cardinal vows, the monk at fault is expelled. It is interesting to note that from the very beginning, and even for lay persons, Buddhism has considered the sexual act to be wrong whenever it causes harm, especially when it is imposed on a child or a sick person. In the West, it seems that most sexual scandals concerning Tibetan teachers are related to some *yogis*. These lay spiritual masters are encouraged to marry. Of course, some system of certification would help, but it is very difficult to set up.

On a practical level, I encourage people who are interested in Buddhism to be more aware of the Buddhist approach to spiritual belief. In exceptional cases, blind faith is okay, but the Buddha himself said, "My teaching should not be accepted out of blind faith, or out of respect for me, but rather by investigation." In the *Maha Anuttara Yoga Tantra* it is stated that before accepting someone as your teacher you should check, test, and thoroughly investigate them—if necessary, for twelve years! The Buddha specified the qualifications required for transmitting the precepts of the *vinaya*, the *sutrayana,* and the lower, middle, and higher *tantras*. If faith alone were sufficient, why would the Buddha have explained all these qualifications?

The spiritual teacher must also remember that being a teacher means serving others. Those who have taken the bodhisattva's vow to liberate all beings should consider themselves to be the lowest beings alive. All the infinite beings are considered our masters. We should serve them, not exploit or bully them.

Some of my friends who follow a Tibetan master recently implicated in some scandal were very worried that such things would be damaging to Buddhism in general. I told them that such things don't matter, ultimately. The *Buddhadharma* has successfully survived for the past two thousand five hundred years. It is solid and very logical. Some scandals here and there, set off by individuals, have happened in the past and may happen in the future. No problem. This will not affect the real Buddhadharma.

Fabien: This is in no way a criticism of the Buddhist religion, which I know and profoundly respect, but somehow I feel uncomfortable when I see, in Nepal for example, so many magnificent Tibetan monasteries. There is a monastery on every corner. It seems paradoxical. Each lama has his own big, beautiful monastery, and just outside the gates there are so many poor people lying in the street with nothing to eat. There are no decent roads, there is no sanitary system, and the water is polluted. I know the lamas cannot resolve the huge problems that strangle Nepal, but I would think it more urgent to feed those who are starving than to build monasteries.

Dalai Lama: I am very much aware of this situation. In our settlements we still need accommodation because there are many students, including nuns and monks, who have no permanent place to stay. But even so, I often say that we should prioritize food and education over shelter, which is just protection against the heat and the rain. "Sooner or later we will have to leave these buildings behind," I say. But despite my advice, some Tibetans—or Tibetan Buddhists—still make their buildings more luxurious than necessary.

Anne: In a way, it was important for the Tibetan community in exile to build monasteries, because the Dharma is the heart of the Tibetan people. The monasteries rapidly become the social center of the exiled community and also house orphanages, dispensaries, schools, and old people's homes. In a way, that justifies their existence.

Dalai Lama: Some people think that a marvelous temple is the Dharma. That is not true. The Dharma is here, in the mind. [He gestures toward his heart.] The worst thing, in the case of Nepal, is that some of these temples are empty. There are no monks, and the few who are there wear sleeves and have long hair. The secretary of the late Karmapa told me very seriously one day, "It is not easy to become a monk. One needs to shave one's head and control one's sex."

Unfortunately, many just shave their hair but don't control the other parts!

Fabien: Is that why you have asked the religious community to pay more attention to social work and education?

Dalai Lama: Yes. I often say that, in these fields, we Tibetans must copy Christian monks and nuns. It is very important. I also tell them, even publicly, that our religious community should decrease in number. I would prefer we had fewer monks and nuns with better motivation and discipline.

A MIDDLE PATH

A Middle Path

Dalai Lama: I would like to go back over something you said. If I understood correctly, although you have a Jewish background, as a result of meeting with Kalu Rinpoche, you developed an interest in Buddhism. I got the impression you were asking whether someone can practice different religions simultaneously. Let me share my thoughts on this. As you may know, I consider the existence of a variety of religions useful for humanity. In the preliminary stages of one's spiritual research, one can practice both Christianity and the Buddhadharma. One can, for example, respect and have faith in the Buddha's teachings on non-violence, compassion, and tolerance, while remaining skeptical about karma and reincarnation, and basically believe in the Creator and feel close to God. At that level, I think it is possible to practice two or even more traditions. It is like being in school: as long as you remain at the general level, you may study a range of subjects. But as you progress to higher studies, you should choose one specialization.

For someone who goes deeper into Buddhist practice, which is based on voidness, interdependence, and no absolute, there is no place for belief in a creator. The opposite is also true. For a Christian, the essential points are the Creator, love of God, and love of fellow human beings. I asked a Christian priest and friend of mine why the theory of rebirth was unacceptable to a Christian of deep conviction. He replied, "The belief that this very life, without any other one preceding it, is created by God is what develops the feeling of intimacy with the Creator." I saw a positive meaning in that. For a genuine Christian, it is not possible to accept rebirth and, even more important for us Buddhists, the belief that everything is interdependent. When you reach a certain level of practice, you have to make a choice. What is your next question?

Fabien: It is about Tibet. Many books have already been written about the Tibetan tragedy. How would you classify the present Tibetan situation? Is there any possibility that you and your people will be able to return to Tibet?

Dalai Lama: The present situation is a kind of stagnation. On my side there is no change. I am still fully committed to the middle approach that I outlined in the Five-Point Peace Plan I presented in Strasbourg in 1989. This approach is based strictly on non-violence, to which my commitment will not change. I bear that responsibility. If the situation becomes uncontrollably violent, my only option is to resign, which is most improbable under the present circumstances.

Fabien: Are you talking about violence in Tibet, or outside?

Dalai Lama: Both. At this moment, there is no hope for meaningful negotiation. The Chinese government is presently adopting an extremely harsh policy toward the Tibetans inside and outside Tibet, as well as against me.

Since 1994, they describe the struggle with the Dalai Lama as war against an enemy. The communist government announced that to kill a snake, one must crush its head. That doesn't matter—I'm still alive and quite active. I'm hoping to live for another thirty or forty years, but I don't know. That is just what I hope.

We all know, especially since the Tiananmen Square massacre, that the spirit of democracy is very much alive in China. This year, on June fourth, which is the anniversary of this event, the Chinese government was exceedingly nervous. This reveals that the desire for democracy is strong. It is only a matter of time. I think a new situation will definitely arise in the next few years. China experts outline three opinions as to what will happen when Deng dies. One group says that as the present leadership is already well entrenched, there won't be much change, and the present policy toward Tibet will continue for at least five or six years. The second notion is that some internal changes will occur. A third opinion foresees a total collapse in China, even civil war. I prefer the second solution.

A total collapse in China similar to that of the Soviet Union in 1991 could easily set off chaos and bloodshed. Given the population of China, any bloodshed would rapidly turn into a major disaster. So, at this moment and in the very near future, there is not much hope of changing China's Tibet policy. But this does not mean there is no hope at all. I believe that, after a few years, the situation in Tibet will have a chance to shift in a positive direction.

The provisions I stated before are based on what the experts say, but as you know we Tibetans have other sources of information, such as oracles, divinations, and astrological studies. The predictions of Padmasambhava and those of some of his authentic followers are really quite remarkable. I have had the opportunity to meet and receive teachings from some of these people. In general, they come very quietly, just like simple pilgrims. They look ordinary, but their spiritual experience is exceptional. So I receive their teachings very discretely. You know, many teachers come to me hinting that I should receive various transmissions from them. This puts me in a difficult position. But the genuinely awakened teachers never act that way. Through other sources, as well as my own divination, we both know the teachings are authentic. Anyway, I really trust their clairvoyance and predictions. According to them, there is hope for the future of Tibet and the Tibetans.

However, if nothing changes for the better in the next ten years, there is a real danger that the Tibetan spirit may disappear *within* Tibet, at least from larger towns like Lhasa. From a numerical point of view, nomads account for the majority of Tibet's population, but people from Lhasa and larger towns are more educated and have a more global vision. If the Tibetan spirit disappears from that more educated community, it will be a great shame.

Fabien: Do you think it will be possible for Tibetan Buddhism to remain and spread in the West, or are there texts, teachers, or sacred objects still in Tibet that are indispensable for its proper transmission?

Dalai Lama: There are several Tibetan Buddhist centers, in the West and outside Tibetan communities, with very wonderful people, who sincerely care for the authentic teachings. These people are very bright, but they are young students. They will need to grow and mature for a few more decades before they can carry the responsibility of transmitting the Buddhadharma from generation to generation. For the moment, Tibetan Buddhism is too young in the outside world.

In the case of Tibetans, they have been immersed in the Buddhadharma since birth, whether they "know" it intellectually or not. For the next two generations, Tibetan Buddhism, which is the most complete form of the Buddhadharma, will be in a delicate situation. In this sense, it is very much linked with Tibetan freedom.

On an individual level, the one hundred thousand Tibetans living in exile can certainly practice and carry on the Buddhadharma. Nothing is missing. If one has sufficient merit and makes the required personal effort, it is possible to achieve buddhahood. But the Dharma needs the support of a community. This is the real question. If Tibet is no more,

I doubt that the one hundred thousand refugees can preserve the Buddhadharma in its totality.

Fabien: Do you feel that what happened to Tibet is part of some kind of historical cycle—a rise and decline of civilizations—or do you think it was an accident?

Dalai Lama: What happened to Tibet? An accident.

Fabien: One has to be realistic. Even when Tibet becomes free, it will never be the same as before.

Dalai Lama: That's right, but I have always distinguished two different aspects in our Tibetan culture: our basic way of life, and the spirit of the Tibetan people. The social system and way of life have completely changed, but I see no need to preserve or restore them. Traditional Tibetan costumes or the way people wore their hair before the Chinese came don't matter. And the Tibetan custom of sticking out one's tongue and scratching one's head as a sign of respect definitely needn't be preserved. These formalities are not necessary, and these parts of Tibetan culture will change. That is fine. However, the other aspects of our culture, the basic, deep, important things—like the Tibetan's spirit of tolerance, humility, and courage—will not change. Their compassionate attitude toward animals, whether they know Tibetan Buddhism or not, is a deeply ingrained habit of my people. For me, these aspects of our culture are truly valuable and worth preserving. My dream is that the Tibet of the future will be an intelligently industrialized nation that will follow a strict program that does the minimum amount of harm to the environment. Respecting the world we live in is an integral part of our Buddhist culture.

You will notice that I make a difference between Buddhist culture and Buddhism. I have often observed that even Tibetans who are *Bön* or Muslim practitioners respect basic Buddhist values. Some of the Tibetan Muslim families—the ones from Ladakh, India, but not those from China—have lived in Tibet for the last four centuries. They have a lot of compassion.

Other Tibetans might choose to be radical atheists. Buddhism is already considered a form of atheism. Even if they have no faith, they can still be influenced by Buddhist culture.

Fabien: It seems young Tibetans are more aggressive in their fight for a free Tibet than those of the older generations.

Dalai Lama: It is not only the younger generation. Let me tell you a story. I once met an old man from Amdo, Eastern Tibet, who had fought in the guerrilla commando units. One day I asked him whether he felt angry toward the Chinese. Before he could even open his mouth to answer, his cheeks were quivering with fury. Finally he blurted out a very aggressive, "Yes!"

Let me tell you another story. In the early eighties I met an old Amdo man who was a very gentle and genuine monk. He must have been around sixty and was very calm and beautiful. We had a long chat about his experiences in the sixties, and he explained to me how the communist Chinese came and destroyed the monastery in which he lived and arrested all the monks. I said, "Yes, that is understandable. The Chinese are very numerous and strong—you were outnumbered." Then I asked what would have happened if the Chinese and the Tibetans had been matched in equal numbers. He answered by gently rubbing circles on one of his palms with the other palm. The meaning of this Tibetan gesture is that the enemy—in this case, the Chinese— would have been wiped out. Tibetans are very gentle and compassion- ate, but they also possess a deep self-assuredness, which is very necessary. Even after living for forty years with Chinese guns pointed at them, the Tibetan spirit has not died. Their patience and non-violence stem not from fear or weakness, but from strength and self-confidence.

Fabien: Have you ever considered going on a hunger strike, like Gandhi did, for the Tibetan cause?

Dalai Lama: Yes, on several occasions I have discussed it, though not a hunger strike to the death. That would be too risky. It could be worthwhile if there were some definite purpose and a fifty-fifty chance of succeeding.

The Tibetan situation is quite delicate. I am just a single Buddhist monk with no special capacity—apart from sincere, altruistic motivation. I have no miraculous or magic power. I never have negative feelings toward the Chinese. If the opportunity arises, I'm determined to help and serve the Chinese, just as I do the Tibetans. That is my only quality. But unfortunately, at the present moment, the Tibetan situation very much depends on me. After some time the Tibetans will be able to carry the load, but for the moment our situation is very fragile, and that load is on my shoulders.

Fabien: There are many different regions in Tibet, and I think it will be necessary for you to stay in power for some time to keep the Tibetan people together. People don't realize how large Tibet is. Regional conflict could easily break out. Don't you think you will continue to play an essential role even in free Tibet?

Dalai Lama: Yes. That is one of the reasons why I have stated that as soon as we return to Tibet, we will set up some form of interim government through an electoral college, not a general election. That government will remain for two years and will organize a general assembly through genuine democratic elections—one person, one vote. As soon as the interim government is established, I will hand over all my political authority. I have officially and formally announced this decision.

It may be that once we get some freedom, bickering will start. When the West was fighting the Eastern bloc, it could forget its own problems. Like when Marshall Tito controlled Yugoslavia, all the people's grievances were suppressed; but as soon as they had some freedom, many problems emerged. Already in the regions of Kham and Amdo, tiny problems create huge fights. Tibetans even kill each other for a small piece of land, while the Chinese stand by watching them. When we get some genuine self-rule, these kind of quarrels are bound to multiply.

Even without any official position, I think my popularity will remain as long as I remain a simple Buddhist monk. If I disgrace myself, then my popularity may diminish, of course! My role could be that of a mediator in conflicts between the government and local people. The judiciary will deal with questions related to sectarianism or regionalism. I would not be in a position to say who is right and who is wrong. Yet, on an emotional level, I think I can say to my people, "Please don't act this way. Please think about Tibet and our future."

Fabien: Since the 1950s, but particularly in recent years, many Chinese of different ethnic groups have relocated to Tibet. Even if Tibet regains its autonomy from China, the Chinese settlers might want to remain in Tibet.

Dalai Lama: According to my middle way approach, they can stay there.

Fabien: But their presence will be another source of conflict.

Dalai Lama: Several aspects of this issue must be considered. The number of non-Tibetans has to be manageable, and those who want to stay must respect Tibetan culture.

Fabien: I sometimes feel that the material world eats up the spiritual world's space. Do you think there is some kind of Manichaean fight between the material and spiritual worlds? I'm thinking, in part, of the plight of your people, as well as that of Native Americans.

Dalai Lama: There are similarities between the Tibetans and the Native Americans, but it is not that simple. The Native Americans have virtually no alphabet or written language, whereas the Tibetan sages have composed whole libraries of metaphysical works.

Our civilization has another thing that is unique. The other day, during the seminar held on my sixtieth birthday in New Delhi, a paper was read by a well-known and highly respected scientist from India. He said that the Buddhadharma, unlike other religious faiths, is based on investigation and respects reasoning and reality. It is very close to scientific thinking. He then quoted some excerpts from Nagarjuna's theory to show how similar it was to modern, subatomic physics and quantum theories. He apologized for his insufficient knowledge of Buddhism, but said that whenever he had the chance to get a glimpse of the teachings of Nagarjuna, he was amazed at how close they were to the most recent scientific discoveries. I felt that if this brilliant scientist had been better acquainted with Buddhism, his view would have been biased. Yet here he was, without the slightest assumptions about Buddhism, and he had immediately seized the essence of its theories.

In 1994, I attended a colloquium with some scientists at Columbia University. A well-known Jewish scientist was telling us how difficult it is to identify reality from the viewpoint of quantum theory. If, as he explained, there is no independent reality and everything comes into being due to many factors, then the scientists' view seems very close to Nagarjuna's theory of emptiness. For Buddhists—at a certain level—the word "emptiness" means the absence of inherent existence.

To return to our earlier point, I respect all other religious traditions. As I mentioned above, millions of people benefit from them. All authentic spiritual teachings have great potential to serve humanity. They all carry the message of love and tolerance. For these reasons, I really respect them. At the same time, I am fully convinced that not all humanity can be religious. Therefore, it is impossible to think that all of humanity will become Buddhist. But this does not prevent me from thinking that the Buddhadharma is the only religion that can work hand in hand with science.

In terms of the Tibetan situation, I feel fully confident that if we educate the Tibetan people properly, we can progress in the material field while still sustaining our spirituality and thus find a harmonious equilibrium.

Fabien: You only partially answered my question. What happens to those groups of people who are much more spiritual, and who give less importance to the material world? History shows that they are always swallowed up by materialists. Consider the Incas and the Native Americans.

Dalai Lama: That was a long time ago. Times have changed. It is true that materialism is based on science, but science is now indicating that other energies, apart from matter, exist. Since science has reached this point, I think a new perspective on the relationship between spiritualism and materialism—or science—is bound to surface.

Fabien: Do you mean that materialism is changing and will become more spiritual?

Dalai Lama: I think so. If spiritualism is too narrow-minded, or confined to blind faith, then of course such a union is difficult. But if we are more spiritually open, then materialism will also open up. That will be a different world. The next century may be very different than this one.

Fabien: Your Holiness, we have discussed some possibilities for change on the global level, and now I would like to discuss topics of a more individual nature, such as daily life, marriage, sex, education, and the media.

In the West it seems as if we try to hide all the bad things in our daily life, a bit like the example of the glass of blood you gave earlier. We are scared of death, we balk at people who are insane or handicapped, or somehow make us uneasy or fearful—

Dalai Lama: Yet, at the same time, on Western television we see nothing but death, violence, blood, mutilation, and killing.

Fabien: That is television, not real life.

Dalai Lama: But it is a picture of humanity.

Fabien: It is not real life, it is like a window. When you go to a funeral, you don't see the body. It is in a box. It is quite similar to the way Siddhartha's father made a great effort to hide the reality of suffering from his son.

These days, people are relying on tranquilizers and antidepressants, instead of trying to work through whatever is bothering them in other ways, like taking a walk, talking to a counselor or friends, exercising, or engaging in spiritual practice. Nowadays, people just take Prozac and other drugs.

Dalai Lama: Do these drugs make you less sensitive? Are they tranquilizers?

Fabien: It seems that when you take Prozac, you stop clinging to the idea that daily reality is negative. It dampens your anguish. What is your opinion about such means of dealing with fear and suffering?

Dalai Lama: Wait. So, essentially people take these drugs to lessen their feelings of mental discomfort, but the result is that they just become less sensitive, less alert? This phenomenon reveals that most of our problems, inside and out, arise from our intelligence. It is the source of our anxiety and mental suffering.

It seems quite foolish to try to eliminate our anxiety by dulling our intelligence. That is really silly! Intelligence is a unique attribute of humanity. There is nothing wrong with intelligence itself. Problems arise when it is not properly guided. Fear, doubt, hatred, and other destructive faculties all come from delinquent intelligence. But why damage the intelligence itself? There are other ways to reduce anxiety and fear. I believe the more attention we give to genuine compassion, the less space there is for fear. Let's develop love and kindness. We will have more self-confidence, more peace of mind.

Fabien: Can you suggest some simple techniques for daily life?

Dalai Lama: A technique that could apply to everyone? I don't know. Peace of mind can be developed through training and daily awareness. It is a question of becoming accustomed to mental training. It takes time. The present generation, as we said, is already polluted because most of its time has been spent catering to negative emotions. It is difficult to go back in time. Intellectually, people may understand that compassion is very good, but how do they make it an integral part of their mind? How long will it take? Fear, doubt, and anxiety have been there for a long time, and the entire society we live in supports the negative side of our intelligence.

People have more opportunities to develop the positive capacities of their intelligence when they are children. We must give young people more opportunities to realize the value of positive intelligence and encourage them in this capacity. While the intellectual side of their personality is developing, a powerful good heart should also be nurtured. When the two are combined—intelligence and a good heart—there is no problem.

Fabien: How can people who are taking Prozac start helping their children develop mental training and compassion when they can't even face their own problems?

Dalai Lama: If, without this medicine, these people are full of hatred and violence, then maybe it is better for them to be dull—slightly—but harmless. Things can be changed. There is hope.

Fabien: Humans tend to avoid taking responsibility for their actions. This attitude causes frustration. If we can at least accept that we are partly responsible, it implies we also have the right and the means to fix the problem. We can try reading your other books, as well as the works of other spiritual leaders and philosophers, but couldn't you give us a clue on how to start cultivating inner peace?

Dalai Lama: For the present generation, the solution lies in the hands of the media. If awareness is heightened and reliable information is made more available, we will possibly begin to perceive our own inner potential, without relying on drugs.

The human being is so wonderful. Properly handled, our intelligence is magnificent. My own experience leads me to think that things are beginning to change for the better. I have recently had more communication with businessmen who are showing an interest in spirituality. Scientists are also more open to things spiritual than they were in the sixties. The more material and scientific development we have, the more science notices its limitations. It is thus compelled to turn to some other option.

Fabien: In the West we tend to look for "easy," external solutions to our problems. We think it is easier to change the outside world than to shift our internal perspective.

Dalai Lama: Exactly. That is the way your society works. Look how you handle disease. The tiny germs are always at fault, aren't they? No one ever considers that the elements of our own body create the possibility for external germs to affect us. If the elements composing our body—earth, air, water, fire, and space—are fit and in balance, then no intruder can establish itself. In the West you rely heavily on external means for everything and completely neglect your own mental potential.

Anne: I think some people take drugs and alcohol because they are afraid of this inner power and prefer to make themselves dull rather than face the endless creativity of a mind they never learned to tame.

What is the deep basis of this fear and anxiety that so many people suffer from?

Dalai Lama: It may be a cultural problem.

Fabien: The fact is, suffering exists and everyone wants to avoid it. That is not a cultural problem. Yet it is true, for many people in the West, that God is the creator and we are his creatures. Not only does this encourage a tendency to be psychologically dependent on someone else, but suffering becomes difficult to explain and even more difficult to accept. Belief in original sin and a culturally instilled feeling of guilt make things even worse.

Dalai Lama: In the Buddhist approach, each being possesses *tathagatagarbha,* or buddha nature. We can all become a buddha. In our deepest nature we are equal to the Buddha. We do not depend on an external entity for good or evil.

In the field of material development, however, we humans have come to a point where we can operate so much from one small switch. Yet we are completely reliant on that switch—on material things, science, and technology. On top of that, scientists have created some false hopes by assuring us that everything can be solved by technology and science. Many factors underlie this present anguish: religious ideology, scientific development, family life, education—

Dalai Lama: Hopefully our next meetings will provide an opportunity to discuss these issues further.

LIVING AND DYING

Living and Dying

Fabien: Your Holiness, I would like to go back over a few points we raised. I was reflecting on compassion being part of our innate nature. For me, compassion is an empty space that creates the possibility of sending a message to another being. For me compassion is always there, within us—

Dalai Lama: What do you mean by saying, "Compassion is always there"?

Fabien: I mean that compassion is a part of human nature. It's not something we have to create.

Dalai Lama: I don't know. [He laughs.] This philosophy is too difficult for me. Compassion is part of our mind.

Fabien: Yes, it is there, inside us. So, the work we have to do—

Dalai Lama: No, No, No! I don't agree! The buddha nature—we are careful to say buddha nature *not* buddha—is innate. Awakening is not innate, but the seed, the potential of enlightenment, is. We can say that compassion is a part of mind, meaning that within our mind compassion can arise. This does not mean that as long as the mind is there—in whatever state—that compassion is also there. That is not true.

Generally speaking, the seed of compassion always exists, but when we are in a state of mind where our hatred is fully developed, we certainly have no compassion. At that time compassion becomes dormant. Two contradictory thoughts or emotions cannot arise in our mind at the same moment. When one is activated, the other is deactivated. In the Buddhist view, a function that is dormant is not referred to as the actual thing.

Fabien: But if we create an empty space within ourselves, that which is dormant can arise. It seems that the key is to let our inner space expand. When we leave some open space in ourselves, does compassion not grow naturally?

Dalai Lama: It is possible. I believe that even people like Hitler, who seemed to be insensible, are capable of feeling some kind of compassion. From what I have read, it seems that when he was with his girlfriend, Eva, and his German shepherd, he would feel "good," meaning he felt less suspicious than usual, allowing some kind of confidence to arise within him. This shows that Hitler also had the seed of compassion. When someone else showed genuine concern or affection for him, he would feel happy.

Fabien: So, if we manage to rid ourselves of negative emotions that prevent this compassion from flowering, it will begin to develop on its own, as soon as it has some space? Even for us, the "lost generation"?

Dalai Lama: Of course. By the way, I'm also a member of this lost generation!

If we make an effort to become aware of our own potential and of the value of compassion, then of course there is a possibility of change, as individuals. As for the world as a whole, I'm not sure. At this moment it seems a bit difficult. We can say that, at the end of the twentieth century, the general conception of humanity and its place in the world is changing very rapidly compared to the past five decades.

Fabien: Popular wisdom says that a person must experience suffering to become a better person. Do you agree?

Dalai Lama: It is not fundamentally necessary. However, it is true that people who have experienced suffering become more mature, more patient. I think the generations who witnessed World War II and the period that followed are in a better position to deal with problems than subsequent generations. They only heard about the war. They didn't experience it directly. Their life has been more smooth. When small difficulties arise, they immediately loose their temper or their patience. They are generally less resilient than their elders. But that does not mean that to become a good person one must suffer. From our Buddhist viewpoint, whether one recognizes it or not, there is always some kind of suffering. The Four Noble Truths outline this: everything is suffering; suffering arises from desire; the cessation of suffering is nirvana; and the eightfold path leads to nirvana.

Fabien: Several times you have mentioned the importance of education. What is the parents' responsibility in educating their children? Is the time parents spend with their children more important for their ethical training than the time the children spend in school? What is more important, the amount of time we spend with our children or the quality of the relationship?

Dalai Lama: Both time and quality of relationship are important. The best solution would be for all the children in the world to attend— and enjoy—schools whose philosophies and programs were rooted in compassion and affection. Children are also entitled to an atmosphere of affection at home. We must build a world in which children can enjoy a positive atmosphere all day long. This cannot be achieved immediately, but we must work toward it. If you can't find a school with good teachers and a proper atmosphere, at least you can try to provide a positive environment at home.

Fabien: What is a good education from a Tibetan point of view? How do you structure lay education in exile? I know that refugee children were sent to various countries for schooling, and then you later resolved not to send them abroad but to keep them within the Tibetan community.

Dalai Lama: That is not quite correct. In the early sixties we used to allow Tibetan orphans to be adopted by foreign families, and a few hundred were adopted in Switzerland. We stopped that practice, except for a few exceptional cases. But we have never prevented Tibetan children from being educated abroad.

Fabien: At what age can a Tibetan child become a nun or a monk? Who chooses, the child or the parents?

Dalai Lama: Generally it's the parents who wish to see their child join the monastery. Novice vows can be taken at the age of seven, but full *bhikshu* ordination can only be taken after the age of twenty. I think we should adopt the system of the Christian nuns and monks, where the candidate is allowed to mature before entering the monastic orders. We should extend the "probation" period. That way, our young people could enter the order knowingly and according to their own decision.

As for our objectives concerning education, I do have a dream. For the past thirty years in India we have tried to give Tibetan children both a Tibetan education—which includes Buddhist philosophy and ethics—and a modern education. We originally thought it would be good to rely almost exclusively on monks and nuns for our teaching staff. The first team of teachers we trained in Kangra, India, included about thirty monks and two nuns. They were subsequently dispatched to teach in the various refugee settlements throughout India. At present, practically none of them are still teaching, which shows how difficult it has been to implement this idea.

We included Buddhist teachings in our school curriculum, but many of the lay teachers had insufficient knowledge of the subject and found it difficult to explain. Even the religious teachers were unable to execute their duty the way I expected. They were just trying to train the brain and were not able to teach students how to integrate the principles of compassion and altruism into their daily life. These must be rooted in the mind in the Buddhist sense of the word. In spite of this, I have noticed that, although children educated in Tibetan schools don't speak English as well as their peers who have been educated in English-style boarding schools, their manners are better.

In our monastic schools students study the most important Buddhist texts. Yet it seems that their minds—and the teachers' minds, for that matter—are impermeable to the texts' meanings. We have a saying: "Leather hardened by butter can never be softened by butter." In Tibet butter is preserved in raw, untanned skins. The leather becomes as hard as a rock and, unlike other skins, cannot be made supple again, no matter how much grease is applied. I sometimes think it is like this with our monastic schools. However, I have noticed that children who have been in contact with Buddha's teachings are more level-headed than those of the same age group who have not. It is even perceptible in their manner of walking and talking. Despite these differences, we still have a long way to go before we can fully realize the educational vision I outlined earlier.

Social environment is also very important when creating educational systems. In our Tibetan schools in India, we find a difference between children who live in boarding schools and those who live in homes with foster parents who genuinely care for them. The children of the latter group are more secure, and their mental state is more calm.

Fabien: When you set up a lay education system in free Tibet, will religious teachings still be part of the curriculum?

Dalai Lama: We are basically a Buddhist community, so, at this point, Buddhist teachings are worked into the curriculum of our schools. In the future Tibet, however, we should have a lay education that is strictly secular. There are many *Bönpos* (followers of pre-Buddhist Tibetan religious traditions) and some Muslim communities. We cannot demand that they study Buddhism exclusively. We will follow the model of different schools and universities around the world. Some subjects will be compulsory, and others will be optional.

Nevertheless, I believe that all Tibetan children—monks, nuns, or lay people—would benefit from learning the basics of dialectic debate, which is a discipline in Tibetan Buddhist monasteries and nunneries. In this tradition, after hearing a lesson on a philosophical subject, students debate on the matter. Each student must first defend one position and then switch positions and defend the opposite reasoning. This sharpens the intellect as well as the mind. This has been introduced into some of our schools in India. It is sweet to see little girls in their school uniforms debating. I requested that these dialectic traditions be introduced into the entire lay community, but unfortunately this seems difficult to implement.

Fabien: It is interesting to observe the role played by the media and other systems of communication in the field of education and family environment. In many households, whether in America or India, television has now become a member of the family. What do you think about its presence in our homes?

Dalai Lama: There's nothing wrong with that. Again, it depends on what you watch. Television is a useful means to gather general information. Of course, people who choose to live in the mountains, like some Christian monks and nuns, and other people whose whole life is devoted to spiritual practice are exceptional cases. They have very little use for television. I visited some monasteries in the south of France where the monks are not allowed to read the newspaper. Buddhist hermits don't need information either. Apart from these cases, I think news is necessary. Programs that show graphic sex and violence and all those films that show how to cheat or steal are not a positive contribution.

But even that depends so much on the viewer. For people who have a proper perspective, such shows can serve as reminders of humanity's negative aspects. When such people see scenes of murder and violence, they will react and say, "Now we have to do something to stop making and selling arms." For others, especially children, such programs may attract and influence them, becoming an example they will follow. This is bad.

Fabien: One problem is the amount of time children spend in front of the television. It can be as much as four hours a day. Their creativity and their studies are negatively impacted by an excess of unnecessary information. Who is to be held responsible for all the moronic and negative messages that TV programs feed our children? Who will have to answer for the negative impact on children's minds?

Dalai Lama: Everyone involved is responsible. For me, anyone who works in the media plays an important role in shaping the minds of our societies. They should definitely develop a greater sense of responsibility instead of thinking only about commercial implications. At my press conferences, I often say how much I appreciate the press with their inquisitive elephant noses. In a democratic country they are often the only ones who can check what is really going on. Without them, many cunning people would escape the law and create a lot of mischief.

I suppose one can argue that media personalities disclose people's private lives, but I feel that someone who is genuine shouldn't have a gap between his or her private and public lives. People should be truthful, and we should apply to ourselves what we say to others. There should be nothing to hide. If important people lead double lives, something is wrong. I basically support the media's point of view on this issue.

At the same time, I am very critical of the careless way the media stirs things up and sensationalizes things. Their success is due to a particular trait of human nature. If a newspaper reports a killing, it creates a shock, and this information is considered "news." If it reports that one thousand old people are being taken care of by compassionate parents or guardians, or if it describes how many millions of children are getting proper loving care from their parents, everyone just thinks, "So what? That is natural. It is nothing new."

As a result, people are beginning to feel that all the media ever talks about is murders, scandals, or catastrophes. This infects us, in a sense, and we get the impression that human nature is hopelessly aggressive and negative. The media should offer us a more balanced view of the world. It would be good to know not only how active our negative emotions are, but also how powerful and effective our positive emotions and actions can be.

Fabien: What about the internet, where people can communicate all over the world about any subject with just a telephone and a computer?

Dalai Lama: I don't know the system well, but I think it can be very positive. Since we are all human beings, we all have the right to know. The main issue with the internet is whether it is used in a positive or harmful way.

Fabien: Another aspect of the internet is that it diminishes the amount of human contact around the world because the medium of exchange is the computer, instead of personal contact, human touch, or hand-written letters.

Dalai Lama: Perhaps, but when there *is* human contact and we don't cultivate a response, then there is no human feeling.

Fabien: Which is the best place to live and raise a family: cities, sub-urbs, or rural environments?

Dalai Lama: Hmm…. What to do? Cities are certainly not our nat-ural environment. In spite of all the facilities the modern world offers, deep down we human beings maintain a close feeling toward plants. We love to have them in our house, even in an artificial form. Our ancestors very much depended on trees for fire, weapons, shelter. They fed on fruit, they wore flowers as decorations and leaves as clothes. Plants are important in our life, and I think there are still traces of that in our genes. From that perspective, it would be better for people to live in small villages, where they could have gardens, rather than in big cities. It would definitely help young people to find some roots.

Fabien: Roots. One cannot mention a child's roots without speaking of family life. Many children suffer as a result of divorce.

Dalai Lama: That is a *real* problem, and it is closely linked to sex. Of course, it is impossible to generalize. There are always exceptional situations where divorce is the better solution. When it is a case involving violence or murder, then it is definitely better to separate the family—to search for a positive, long-term solution to such domestic problems.

Divorce seems especially frequent in America. I've observed several couples who have this hobby. Over the years, they get married, have children, divorce, marry again, have more children, divorce again, and so on. It must be very difficult, even from an economic point of view. The worst thing is that most of the children whose parents divorce are scarred for life.

Most people don't seem to realize how crucial real marriage is. Mad love is not enough. In a real marriage, the couple should base their love not just on attraction but also on mutual understanding and genuine respect, rooted in an appreciation of each other's qualities. A sense of commitment and responsibility will naturally follow. A relationship founded on these elements can make for a truly happy marriage, one that will probably last many years, if not for their whole life.

Now sex. From the Buddhist viewpoint, sex is natural. Its main purpose is, of course, reproduction. Sex is something we have in common with animals. They are less intelligent, so they follow nature's laws more simply. Because of their intelligence—ha!—human beings seek pleasure for the sake of pleasure, not realizing how temporary it is, and introduce complications. Sometimes their sex life becomes a bit extreme or perverted, especially in the West, with so much "sexual freedom." But one can't say it makes us very free. Don't you find that certain aspects of the Western way of life actually promote sex? In itself, sex is not wrong, but I think it is like drinking: it becomes a problem when it is excessive. In its normal context sex is not a problem, but it definitely becomes a source of difficulties and suffering when it gets too complicated or extreme and lacks self-discipline. This is due both to our tendency to be dissatisfied and to the environment we have created for ourselves, where sexual stimulation is quite excessive.

I have a very sad story of some Western friends who used to come to see me in Dharamsala. They were such a close family. Just recently I heard that the father sexually abused his daughter. The parents divorced. The daughter was so traumatized that now she lives in a mental hospital. Such awful examples show that, although sex in itself is normal, it can cause terrible suffering when it gets out of control. I think this is a field in which it is very important to have both self-discipline and awareness.

Fabien: I'm not sure that sexual excess or perversion is a very good example of human intelligence.

Dalai Lama: It is a corrupt form of intelligence. That is why it is important to warn children about sexuality and explain to them that excessive sexuality has many negative consequences. Children should learn this as early as possible.

We had some discussions about introducing sex education into Tibetan schools. The question arose because some of the girls were getting pregnant. Some people said that, if you tell children about sex, such problems will get worse. It is difficult to judge. Some youngsters don't know anything about sex and act secretly, with undesirable consequences. On the other hand, publicly announcing how to use condoms might encourage them to be more careful, though perhaps more sexually active than they would normally be.

Fabien: What do you say to young Tibetans concerning condoms and sex?

Dalai Lama: I believe that family planning and birth control are very important. Regarding the system of birth control we choose, we must think carefully and find a non-violent system. If we take a pill that expels the egg once conception has taken place, that is killing.

Fabien: That is difficult because most people don't really know the effect of the different contraceptive pills available to women. In what cases is abortion justified?

Dalai Lama: From the Buddhist point of view, only in very rare and exceptional cases, or when the mother's life is in danger.

Anne: What if a women becomes pregnant through rape?

Dalai Lama: That is really difficult. Rape is a form of sexual misconduct. It always leads to tremendous suffering. That is a very difficult situation. Then later there is an unwanted child. What to do?

Fabien: When abortion is a case of conscience, who decides? Is the life of the child in the mother's hands, the father's hands, the doctor's, or the state's?

Dalai Lama: I think the most important voice should be given to the mother. She has more right to decide than anyone else because she has to bear the child for nine months. The father didn't do much, did he? The mother carries the child for nine months, gives birth to it, and feeds it with her own milk.

Anne: Despite having other means to avoid pregnancy, some women have repeated abortions, which is a very violent and traumatic way of dealing with the situation. People are now beginning to realize how traumatic abortion can be. I feel that women who choose abortion are not aware of the consequences of this act, for the unborn child and for themselves.

Dalai Lama: Yes, as a Buddhist, I have to say abortion is wrong, but it is up to the individual to decide. The mother who aborts must know that is a negative act, but we cannot punish her for that. It is an individual right.

Anne: Are you saying that a woman has the right to kill, whereas for anyone else killing is a crime?

Dalai Lama: That is very difficult! I think the logic goes like this. If there is a positive goal and a sincere, pure motivation, then even killing is permissible. Basic Buddhist teaching states that, under particular circumstances, violence is permissible. Such examples are seen in the Buddha's own life stories.

Let's take the case of a family where the mother is expecting a seriously handicapped child. One must weigh the different aspects, the difficulties the child will have to face, its capacity or incapacity to make any spiritual progress, the problems the parents will have to face, especially if the child is going to be a major obstacle to their spiritual practice and progress. If one eliminates one being out of compassion, with concern and deep prayers for it to have a better reincarnation, then the negative act of elimination is combined with a sincere motivation so that all those involved can continue toward the right goal. On the contrary, if, to avoid killing, we do something that allows a lot of negative consequences to develop in relation to our spiritual path, the end result may be even more negative. If one chooses abortion because of money or other superficial reasons, it is very hard to condone such a decision.

Speaking more generally, when a person is in a coma and a huge machine is needed just to keep her or him breathing—without any hope of recovery—I think it is more positive to switch the machine off, especially when it is very expensive and the rest of the family is in a precarious situation. Whether the person is rich or poor, if the brain is no longer functioning and the person is kept alive artificially, what's the use? It would be better for the family to spend that money on a positive project in the field of education or medicine. The crucial point is to have pure motivation.

Fabien: Problems of abortion and mercy killing or euthanasia need careful reflection so that the laws we make don't oppose our inner laws as human beings. The law might say that abortion is okay, but deep inside many people feel it is wrong. In some countries mercy killing is legal, while in others it is severely condemned. How can we ever make universal laws about the right to live and the right to die?

Dalai Lama: Concerning abortion and mercy killing, it is quite simple. In general, I think both should be avoided. If they become legal, then at least open discussion is possible. If the law deems such acts illegal, then even the exceptional cases cannot be compassionately dealt with. These are difficult social and ethical domains.

Fabien: From what you said earlier, it seems that there are important karmic and spiritual connections between the members of the same family. Knowing that our relationships are conditioned by things we did in previous lives makes it easier to deal with such family situations. It prevents a lot of anger, resentment, and violence. However, it bothers me when people shrug off their responsibility, saying, "It's karma." I think it is exactly the opposite. Believing that each act produces consequences can only increase our sense of responsibility. The Buddhist vision of rebirth makes this life seem more valuable, not less. If I didn't believe that, I would have no way to understand my life, no indication about positive ways to deal with difficult situations.

Dalai Lama: This God knows.

Fabien: What?

Dalai Lama: God knows the reason. [He laughs.]

Fabien: But I don't, so it doesn't help.

Dalai Lama: Those who believe in God accept that his ways are mysterious. By believing that, they also get some consolation. They can think, "The situation is very bad, but there must be some divine purpose in it." Then their suffering has some meaning. It is just another way of seeing things.

Fabien: But the theory of rebirth is not intended to give consolation. It is a way to make people more responsible.

Dalai Lama: What I meant was that if one accepts that there is a creator, then that view also offers us a way to accept the different situations that arise in our life. It is never easy to face tragedy. On a conventional level you feel very bad, but you can believe that even suffering is created by God.

Anne: Doesn't that present the risk of making us feel victimized, consciously or subconsciously—forced to accept the situation because God sent it to us? Believing in karma gives us a greater sense of our own responsibility. If something happens to me, it is because I did something that produced this result. If I am responsible for the cause, then I am also an agent of change.

Dalai Lama: That's right. For Buddhists or some Hindus who believe in karma, that is the explanation. You don't need to explain that to *me!*

Fabien: We know that you know that, but I think it is useful to mention it.

Dalai Lama: Fabien, the book that will be made from these interviews is intended for a wide public. You cannot assert these things.

Fabien: Yes I can! Someone once said that it is better to live just three days believing in reincarnation than three full lives without believing in it. Believing in karma is just a different way of seeing things. My opinion on this subject is not rooted in Buddhism alone. As a businessman, I believe that my actions will have results. It seems to be a very intelligent system.

Dalai Lama: But that is your private, individual experience.

Fabien: Yes, but I can at least be an example, no more than that. I know that throughout these interviews you have been mainly intent on defending the Christians. Let me try to support the Buddhists.

Dalai Lama: Ha, ha, ha! That is a good exchange! All right, the rebirth theory may widen our perception, but I feel the Buddhist concept of looking at the whole of humanity and all other living creatures as individuals who were, are, or will be our mother—what we call "all mother sentient beings"—is much more important. Of course, since I am a Buddhist, my viewpoint is slightly biased. However, I find that just hearing or saying those words produces tremendous openness. Thinking of human beings alone is a bit narrow. To consider that all sentient beings in the universe have been our mother at some point in time opens a space of compassion.

But please understand me. I do not want to give the impression that we are trying, with more or less subtlety, to imprint a Buddhist message in people's minds. We decided to base our discussion on secular ethics, as simple human beings, according to innate human feelings. This should remain our basis for explaining compassion and other such concepts. At its core, it should have nothing to do with religion.

Fabien: You are perfectly right. Change doesn't have to start with reasoning extracted from complicated religious concepts. But how can we define "right living" from a point of view that is not specifically Buddhist?

Dalai Lama: Beyond any Buddhist viewpoint, I think that those actions that ultimately bring happiness are right actions, while those actions that ultimately bring pain are wrong. The threshold between right and wrong is pain. Bad and good can be measured by our experience of suffering and happiness. But this means we must observe and think carefully. Let's not mistake temporary pleasure for lasting happiness. Many people have ended up in prison because of a few fleeting moments of pleasure, haven't they?

Fabien: That raises another important issue: jail. When a person slips and breaks a leg, he is taken to the hospital and cared for until he is cured. But when people commit moral slips or make other illegal mistakes, they are taken to jail where nobody tries to heal them. Inmates rarely get medical or psychological help. Many lives end at the prison doors. Shouldn't society try to heal morally injured people before, or even after, they become delinquents?

Dalai Lama: There are people who have created movements and organizations around these issues. I was invited to the Tihar Jail in Delhi once—I wanted to see what the physical and mental conditions were like—but at the last minute the home ministry rescinded the invitation. I guess they were not ready to have me visit. I also met some Americans who were taking care of prisoners. These people, as well as the prison manager in Delhi, told me it really helps prisoners when we tell them that they deserve attention, that they should not feel rejected by society, and that they are not hopeless. We have to help enforce the idea that people can change and we are there to help them. This can influence prisoners' attitudes a lot and gives them incentive to reform. In some cases they teach prisoners to practice some short prayers or meditation techniques. Apparently it is really helpful.

Fabien: There are many non-profit organizations that try to help prisoners, but isn't it basically the government's job to integrate prisons into society? Why do we always have to push our governments into action?

Dalai Lama: I have more trust in people. Governments are always changing.

Fabien: What do you think about the death penalty?

Dalai Lama: Very bad! The death penalty is used in two ways: dissuasive and punitive. The other day, the BBC broadcast a story about an eighty-four-year-old man in England who was originally from Russia. He was persecuted by a Nazi many years ago and is now trying to bring the Nazi to court. That is merely revenge. There is no longer any reason to be fearful of these individuals. Those who want these people "brought to justice" really want to savor revenge. It is absolutely unnecessary.

Fabien: Then what do you suggest we do with the people who participated in the Holocaust, or the murder of countless people in Chile, Cambodia, or the Soviet Union under Stalin, even if these events happened decades ago?

Dalai Lama: It is better to pardon. Not forget, but forgive. The deeds such people did were hateful, negative, worthy of being condemned, but they belong to the past. Ultimately, all people deserve compassion and, when necessary, pardon.

Even as a preventive measure, I'm not at all convinced that the death penalty has any value whatsoever. If a young person became a criminal through lack of love and affection, more hatred is not going to make the situation right. If there really existed a young criminal who we were absolutely certain could never change for the better, whether by spiritual means, meditation, or whatever—if we were absolutely sure that by remaining alive he or she would only murder more people—then perhaps we should consider it. But I still cannot believe that capital punishment would help. There must be other means.

I think jails are necessary. It's the public's attitude toward prisoners that needs to change. It should be more positive so as not to reject or exclude people who are, or have been, in jail.

Fabien: But petty delinquency mainly concerns young people whose first "crime" is very often just a slip that is not very serious. Putting these youngsters in jail with hardened criminals does not help them. I think it would be more constructive to focus their time on community service and other social work, rather than just sitting in a cell, surrounded by other unhappy people.

Dalai Lama: Definitely. If a young person's fault is small or reparable, and if putting him in jail destroys all hope of reintegrating him into society, then social work would definitely be a better solution.

Fabien: Now I would like to speak about sports.

Dalai Lama: Sports? I'm an expert at sports. Zero every time!

Fabien: Do you think sports can replace war?

Dalai Lama: In a way, yes. It occupies people mentally and physically. But then, sports hooligans create many small wars!

Fabien: In large stadiums, one sees up to a hundred thousand people stamping and screaming to support a few dozen men who are running around on the field. On the one hand, this is a good way to release tension and express emotions; but, on the other hand, our passion for sports often resembles a neurosis that just reinforces competition and negativity.

Dalai Lama: Both are possible, but I prefer to see sports as another field where human beings can use their intelligence and creativity.

Fabien: What about music?

Dalai Lama: Human emotions are shaped not only by thought, but also by other mediums such as voice and sound. I think all forms of music, vocal or instrumental, have an influence on our emotions. Throughout the world musicians use this knowledge. Louder, more hectic sounds convey fear or wrath, while soft music is soothing. There is a difference between reciting *mantras* and chanting them. Chanting effects the emotions much more. The words and the meaning are the same, but the tune acts to connect us more deeply, especially in the case of devotional prayers.

Fabien: In Tibet, art—like music and writing—was reserved for sacred purposes. I heard that Tibetan artists could neither change the traditional style nor invent a new one, and that the proportions were sacred and immutable. What about art in the future Tibet?

Dalai Lama: The inertia of Tibetan art was mainly caused by a lack of initiative and creativity. In the case of the Fifth Dalai Lama, for instance, I don't think one can speak of creativity. For me, the word "creativity" evokes modern artists who imagine something entirely new and then express it. The Fifth Dalai Lama's visions belong to quite a different dimension. First, the visions appeared before him. He would clearly see some great lamas, certain valleys, specific instruments or objects. Then he described his visions to his artist, or may even have painted them himself, but the result was a faithful copy of what he saw. Would one call that creativity?

I find it risky to establish a parallel between a mystical experience and creativity. The painter drew the face of a wrathful deity the way the Fifth Dalai Lama described it. It then became a tradition. That is not creativity. But Tibetan history has also been graced by great artists and painters who showed wonderful creativity in developing new techniques and styles. We had great masters, such as those of the Karma Gadri school, and artists who perfected the Lungboum and Petri styles using wonderful colors and techniques.

I see two ways of preserving Tibetan art in the future. One is to copy previous masters meticulously, and the other is to use existing techniques to create new expressions according to our present social life and experience. I think new styles should develop, and I have made this appeal to my people. In fact, we recently had some artists from Tibet show their paintings here in Dharamsala. Some were related to the Dharma, but others were closer to modern art.

Fabien: All of these questions relate to how humans create, mold, and live within their environments—both physical and spiritual. In relation to this, I would like to ask you about health. In the Tibetan medical system is health linked more to mental or to physical factors?

Dalai Lama: They carry the same weight. Problems in our physical body affect clarity of mind. Often there is nothing wrong with the body, but some event related to our mental or emotional make-up causes us to be ill.

Fabien: What is the basis of good health?

Dalai Lama: The human body is composed of the elements I mentioned earlier: air, fire, earth, water, and space. By their very nature, these elements conflict with each other. Fire is hot, water is cold, earth is solid, and air is light. They are opposites. If they were not in conflict, there would be no progress. Our Tibetan system of philosophical debate is similar to this: it provokes a lot of contradiction. As a result, real knowledge or wisdom can develop. Without contradiction there would be no further development. Health occurs when these contradicting elements that compose our body remain in a state of balance. Even if external germs or viruses enter our body, our immune system will function perfectly as long as our inner elements are in harmony. The body itself has a natural ability to fight external aggression. But when there is disharmony among the elements, external aggressors find a space they can invade.

Fabien: To which medical system do you entrust your health?

Dalai Lama: I have always found holistic medical systems, which consider the body, the mind, and the environment together, more useful than medical systems that separate these elements of our being—especially for long-term or chronic diseases. After having successfully tried it on myself for many years, I have developed great—almost blind—faith in the efficacy of Tibetan medicine. I'm very skeptical about allopathic medicine, although I realize that it is wonderful in emergency cases. When I get a high fever, for example, of course I'm quite willing to take an allopathic treatment, like aspirin.

Fabien: So, for immediate relief, you think allopathic treatment can help, but you don't trust it to restore deeper balance on a long-term basis?

Dalai Lama: Exactly. For the latter, I prefer Tibetan medicine. It really works. It is a bit demanding, in the sense that one has to take the treatment for several months, and the medicines and doses need to be adjusted quite often according to the body's response to these treatments. But it is really effective in keeping the elements in harmony.

Fabien: Do you think it would be positive for all the medical systems in the world to work together and share their knowledge?

Dalai Lama: I definitely think so. In particular, I think Chinese and Tibetan medicine, as well as the Muslim Unani system of the Afghans and the Indian Ayurvedic system, should work together.

Fabien: What about African medical systems?

Dalai Lama: I think we should discern two categories of traditional medicine: the systems that have fundamental written texts with explanations and commentaries, such as Chinese, Tibetan, or Ayurvedic medical sciences; and indigenous medical knowledge that has been orally transmitted over generations. For example, my mother knew a lot of family remedies that were common knowledge for Tibetans who were raised in Tibet and who were familiar with Buddhist traditions. This practical wisdom is not based on the same kind of knowledge that Tibetan doctors are required to master during their approximately twelve years of formal study.

Many African languages were not written down and their knowledge, vast as it may be, is based on oral transmission alone. Their indigenous medical knowledge operates similarly. It is surely valid, but cannot be put on the same level as literary knowledge.

The Tibetan tradition, based on Buddhist knowledge of the five sciences, including medicine, logic, and philosophy, is completely capable of engaging in a dialogue—as an equal—with modern science. Thanks to this interface, I think we will be able to preserve Tibetan culture while increasing our scientific knowledge. Oral traditions, like those of the Native Americans or Africans, exist in a different category of debate.

Fabien: What advice would you give to doctors, nurses, or others working with sick people?

Dalai Lama: I consider these professions the most precious in the world. These people do a great service to humanity. Those who come to them in pain, in desperation, are facing a situation that is beyond their own control, and they have tremendous expectations in relation to these medical practitioners. The vast majority of helpers in this field are truly devoted to their work. Logically, the more they realize how much their patients depend on them, the more their healing power increases. They can think, "These people come to us with such hope and expectation. Even a small, warm smile will bring great comfort. One kind word can make such a difference, even when the situation is really hopeless."

Although it is important to be truthful, that doesn't mean one should be rough, insensitive, or even too frank. When I am in the hands of a doctor who is smiling and concerned, I feel this doctor will really take good care of me. I've met doctors with sophisticated machines who showed no human feeling. It made me feel strange. They may have been great professionals, but they did not inspire me with confidence.

Fabien: Death is also difficult, both for dying people and their families, and also for medical practitioners. Now there are many associations that teach ordinary people and professionals to communicate with near-death patients, using massage, therapeutic touch, and other methods. This is very useful. We used to think the priest was the only one allowed to help during the last moments of life. But these days, there are fewer priests and people are less religious, so we need to fill this gap, don't you think?

Dalai Lama: Sogyal Rinpoche's book, *The Tibetan Book of Living and Dying,* talks about this. On a human level, beyond any religious context, I think a dying person naturally appreciates the presence of friends who show concern and share in the unfortunate period he or she is going through. The dying person will feel less alone. He will still know he is dying, but he will feel happier. Imagine another person in the same situation, alone, behind a shut door. How sad he might feel!

Fabien: Why do we have such difficulty facing death? Why do we refuse to accept this fundamental reality of life?

Dalai Lama: It is always better when both the living and the dying accept this necessary end. But whatever the case, we should try to make the end full of peace and affection. One of my friends, a deputy and monk from Ganden Monastery, came to see me two days ago. He has incurable stomach cancer. Now that his illness is clearly diagnosed, he has decided that there is no hope and that it is time to go. When we met, he was not even upset. I told him, "If you recover, that is good. If you die, that is also good. Now the time has come to think about your next life." I even joked with him. Not only is this man a great scholar, but he is also a good monk and an excellent chant master with a wonderful voice. So I proposed, "Until you reach buddhahood, you should be a chant master, as well as a *geshe* (the Tibetan equivalent of a doctor of philosophy) and a good monk." He promised to do so.

Of course, we both felt that he was departing imminently, but in spite of that he was still very happy. I could see no sign of worry. Such is the result of practicing the Dharma, of believing in rebirth, and of having buddhahood as a target. Whether these things are true or not, they are a great psychological help. Imagine how difficult it must be for someone who doesn't believe in rebirth, but thinks that his or her only life is now coming to an end. And after? Nothing. Nothing to trust, nothing to believe in. It must be terrible. If he or she believes in God, at least there is some basis for hope.

At the time of death, the best parting gift is peace of mind. Knowing this can provide health professionals with a wider perspective on death. They must be open to the fact that people depend on them at this very special moment of their lives, so they should act with a greater sense of responsibility and compassion. It can make a big difference. Helping people at the moments of birth and death is one of the most valuable services we can render to humanity.

It's true that in the West people generally avoid thinking about dying and death. Do they act this way in order to protect their happiness? I find this infeasible. If they feel anxious whenever they are confronted with an event they perceive as negative, then surely it is much better to learn to face that event, to think about it, to look at it openly, and become acquainted with it. The more we reflect on old age and death, the more we see it as a natural process. It is nothing extraordinary. If we prepare ourselves in this way, then when such events actually happen, the work of accepting them as a very normal part of our life is already done. We can simply think, "Now the period where my life ends is coming." I think that is a better approach.

Fabien: And what about children, in this case?

Dalai Lama: It's difficult to say. When they are young, before the age of seven or eight, they have not finished developing their powers of reasoning, and direct contact with death may shock them. I feel it is better to avoid any form of trauma at this age.

When we were still in Tibet, my youngest brother, Tenzin Chogyal, and I used to go with our mother to circumambulate the Norbulinka, the summer palace in Lhasa. There was a pavilion filled with wonderful collections of books in the garden where the Thirteenth Dalai Lama used to stay in retreat. One day a stuffed tiger that someone brought from India was spread across the veranda. When my little brother saw it, he was so frightened that he fainted. From that day on he refused to go near the veranda. It was no use trying to persuade him that it was not a real tiger and that it could not harm him. Once a child has been shocked, logical explanations cannot help.

Fabien: Western children see death all the time on the TV. Still, it is not the same as being in the presence of a dead person, which can be a shock. A lot depends on the family context. If a child has seen his grandfather grow old and then die, he might accept death as a natural process. This can be a way to explain death, the comfort of prayer, the difference between body and mind.

Dalai Lama: I would still be very hesitant about exposing children younger than eight to the shock of death, when possible. After that, their way of thinking changes and the shock is not the same.

Fabien: One last question about health and dealing with death. Do you think that a short period of daily yoga or meditation can contribute to good health and help prepare us—ultimately—for death?

Dalai Lama: Many people have told me that. I wonder. Peace of mind definitely contributes to good health; but meditation, for most people, means thinking of nothing, just relaxing into some kind of thoughtless state. That can help a little in sustaining peace of mind, making it deeper and longer lasting. At least, during that moment, the turbulence of the mind subsides. Meditation appears to help, but it is just a means. Actual peace of mind is the main point.

I find the most effective way to achieve peace of mind is through analytical meditation. We have already mentioned some different aspects of this, such as reflecting on death and accepting it as part of our life. If, on top of that, we have deeply reflected and gained knowledge on subjects such as rebirth, ultimate buddhahood, and the nature of *samsara* (temporal, unenlightened existence), then death is nothing more than changing clothes. All these types of meditation are means with which to analyze reality. As true awareness of these things grows in us, the reasons to worry cease to exist.

Fabien: Is death the most important moment of one's life? You said that birth and death are crucial moments, but at the time of birth we are hardly conscious, whereas at the time of death, or just after, we can—

Dalai Lama: After death, you can't remember either.

Fabien: I was hoping there might be some consciousness then, too.

Dalai Lama: Yes, at death you have more worry and more pain because of that consciousness. According to those who accept rebirth, the moment of death is extremely important. It is the last moment of preparation for our next life. Therefore we should develop a very positive attitude grounded in a peaceful mind at that time.

In Buddhism, our daily practice is a continual reminder of the fact of death. It is also a preparation for the death process itself. Every deity yoga practice contains sections that refer to the death process. The "eight stages" of this practice refer to the dissolving of the inner elements: earth, water, fire, air, and space. These elements contain three more aspects, for a total of eight. During the last stage of death, the mind, although still present, becomes completely independent from the body. Consciousness remains through the first four stages; then we enter a level that is beyond consciousness and within which there are three further stages. For a Tibetan Buddhist, the *powa*, or release of consciousness, ritual precludes this phase. As long as consciousness remains, we must try to think about emptiness and bodhicitta and remember the guru and the Buddha, Dharma and Sangha, so that the last moments of this life are impregnated with a positive state of mind. The immediate effect is a rebirth that is positive.

Death is important from another point of view. Birth is the result of our previous lives. Whether we like what we got, or not, it is too late. Our rebirth is not in our own hands. Whether we are a girl, a boy, a European, a Tibetan, or an Indian, the situation has already ripened. Well, I've heard that nowadays one can change one's sex, but I don't see the use of it. Even if a man can become a woman, he still can't become pregnant.

Fabien: Not yet.

Dalai Lama: That's right, not yet. Soon we can add that to the long list of our worries, but we still won't have the power to change our overall rebirth situation, whereas at the moment of death the power to choose your next destination is still in your hands. That is why this time is so crucial. Unfortunately, we do not have the power to stop time.

MIND AND MIRACLES

Mind and Miracles

Fabien: One hears incredible stories about Tibet and the Tibetan teachers in exile. As soon as Tibet is mentioned, stories of miracles, large and small, crop up. How do you explain these phenomena? What is it that makes Tibet such a strange and powerful country?

Dalai Lama: There must be a basis for a miracle to happen. Without grounding there is no miracle. If you know something about how these phenomena arise, then what seems extraordinary to others is normal for you, isn't it?

Let's take the example of the rainbows and circles of light that appear at the time of a great lama's passing. We Tibetans know that these phenomena express the high level of spiritual experience that the person has reached. During such events some mysterious forces such as *khandroma* (feminine deities) and other spirits gather. Then, as I have already said, rainbows, which are related to rain and temperature, will appear. All these different factors combine to produce what people call a miracle. People who know about interconnected causes find such events more normal. People who have no knowledge of interdependence, or no idea of the different causes and effects in play, just see the rainbows and the body of this great being without seeing the connection between the two. To them it is a miracle. For them a person who can fly is also a miracle.

A few years ago an old nun came to see me. For many years she lived in a shack here in Dharamsala. She was about eighty when she passed away. Before dying she came to offer me two ancient texts on *Dzogchen* (Great Perfection) *trekchö* and *tögal*. They were very beautiful texts composed by Tsogtrug Rangdrol, a great teacher. I inquired about her life story. When she was twenty-six or so, she lost her two children, and shortly thereafter her husband died. At that point she gave up, left her family—which was quite wealthy—and began living like a beggar, visiting all the sacred places.

Eventually she reached Drikung Monastery. Behind the monastery there is a high mountain. A very old Dzogchen lama from Kham (eastern Tibet) lived up there. He had about fifteen disciples. One day this nun saw one of them fly from one side of the mountain to the other. "He just opened his red shawl like wings and flew," she told me. I thought to myself, "this old nun on the verge of death, who has lived in Dharamsala for fifteen years as a beggar and is considered to be clairvoyant, has absolutely no reason to lie to me." I took her statement as truth.

Such things may seem strange at first, but for us they are quite possible. The body is composed of the five elements. The element of consciousness, even in an ordinary state, is superior to the others. However, a normal person's consciousness never functions at its full capacity, since its potential is not fully developed. When, through meditation, all the forces of the mind are correctly channeled and eventually gain more strength, they assume the full scope of their capacities and can control the other elements. According to this theory, through certain meditation techniques the breath can be stopped or controlled and one can levitate. Some practitioners can even fly. These accomplishments are simply due to training and to our mastery of specific techniques. To someone who has no idea about the subject, however, they look like miracles.

Fabien: Does that mean a person who can fly is a highly realized being? Are these powers signs of spiritual realization?

Dalai Lama: In a way they go together. In the case of Milarepa, the famous Buddhist poet, saint, and visionary, these qualities were achieved as a by-product of his meditation on the clear light. His goal in meditating on the clear light, his main practice, was to increase infinitely the wisdom that understands emptiness. But, in fact, once you develop deeper experience about the innermost, subtle consciousness—what we call the clear light—these miraculous powers arise.

Fabien: One has the impression that authentic practitioners don't really care about these "supernatural" abilities.

Dalai Lama: That's right, it is normal for them. I'll give you an example. A team of doctors from Harvard Medical School lead by Dr. Herbert Benson carried out experiments on the physiological capacities of three Tibetan practitioners who used to live and practice in the Himalayas. They found that these yogis manifested extraordinary capacities in that they could maintain stable body temperatures even when placed for several hours, naked, in extremely cold chambers. These results were even reported in the *Journal of Medical Sciences.* In fact, these three practitioners had never made any particular effort to develop the technique of inner heat, or *tummo,* as we call it. They just meditated on *shunyata,* or emptiness, and practiced deity yoga. The capacity to maintain inner heat had developed as a by-product of their mastery of deity yoga.

Fabien: There are also many stories about the marvelous signs that appear at a tulku's birth.

Dalai Lama: Some stories tend to exaggerate such matters, though others are true.

Fabien: Are there always exceptional signs at the time of a tulku's birth?

Dalai Lama: Not necessarily. All this must seem very strange to people who have no knowledge of Tibetan history, religion, or culture.

For many years, the geographical isolation of Tibet added to its mystery. What was normal for us was entirely new to the modern world. When my country became accessible, all these strange stories spilled out. People were very curious. Some outsiders developed a genuine interest in understanding our spiritual sciences.

Once, when I was visiting Eastern Europe—Poland or Czechoslovakia —I had the opportunity to visit a science laboratory where they had carried out many experiments on mental capacities and clairvoyance. One person I met told me that through sheer concentration it is possible to displace an object by a few centimeters, without touching it. In this case, I think it is a result of sheer concentration, backed up by capacities that are probably connected to certain aspects of the person's previous life. These people probably don't know how and why they can do such things.

Fabien: There are many theories explaining these phenomena, but very few people can really control both mind and matter.

Dalai Lama: There may be quite a simple explanation for this. As you know, I've never considered myself a healer. I have no such quality. I'm a simple Buddhist monk who is just beginning, with great difficulty, to reach buddhahood. But if I take ordinary, pure water and recite some mantra in front it, the water seems to acquire the power to help some people. At times I'm in a hurry and the recitation is not quite perfect, but I always do it with sincere motivation and it still helps. Obviously, the other person's attitude is important, too. It has to do with their receptivity and perhaps our karmic links. Such things seem strange or miraculous—but are they really?

Fabien: What do you think about scientists who study the brain and the mind? You, as well as they, seem to think that everything can be explained.

Dalai Lama: That's right. This reminds me of an Indian friend of mine who is a Buddhist. He started out as a university professor and then became a monk. He is especially interested in emptiness. I had great respect for him and permitted him to live here with my monks. Later he disrobed. He was spoiled by one Western woman! (I'm just teasing, of course—breaking his monk's vows was his own decision.) This man practiced a lot and continues to be a very good Buddhist. One day we were joking. He said that he had made more progress in his practice of emptiness after disrobing. I replied, "In that case, we should all follow your example." We laughed.

One day he made an interesting remark. "Buddhism begins where science ends," he said. There is some truth in that. Science is highly developed as far as matter is concerned, but it stops when it reaches into the dimensions of the mind. Buddhism starts with the mind.

Anne: Mind is immaterial, which makes it fundamentally different from matter. Does mind obey the same laws of interdependence and karma that uphold the material world? Do the principles of karma and interdependence function the same way for mind as they do for matter?

Dalai Lama: They apply to the mind and its actions. Of course, one cannot explain the mind in terms of parts and directions in space, as we do in the case of material things. In the latter, we split the whole into its parts and we can explain the interdependent nature of the whole from this more fragmented perspective. We cannot do that for the mind. In this case, interdependence is explained in terms of time and its divisions. Otherwise it is the same.

Fabien: So space becomes time.

Dalai Lama: The mind, time, and everything that has continuity can be divided into moments. Yet when we say, "mind," we don't think in terms of today's mind, yesterday's mind, or tomorrow's mind. Rather, we refer to something we consider mind itself. But if we look closely, mind itself cannot be found. Even the shortest moment has a beginning and an end. If there were no beginning and no end, then there couldn't be a continuity.

Anne: If mind itself cannot be found, how does it interact with matter?

Dalai Lama: Now this is the problem. Within the scope of my small understanding—according to the higher tantras in general and the *Kalachakra* in particular—the five elements function on several levels. On an external level, they constitute the material world. On an internal level, we are composed of the same five elements, which function on three other levels: the gross physical level; a more subtle level we might call energy; and the innermost, subtle mind or clear light that contains the *nuspa*, the potential, or most subtle energy, of those same five elements. The clear light aspect of the mind is called "the creator of all phenomena existing within the circle of existence (samsara) and beyond." There is a connection between the inner level and the most subtle consciousness, so that when some action arises in the latter, it can influence the elements in their subtle aspect. These, in turn, influence the less refined elements.

But for me, neither the mind nor external particles have any origin, because it is virtually impossible to prove they do. We prefer to say that space particles are beginningless. Trying to defend the opposite approach is not only very difficult, but it also creates a lot of complications.

So we choose to accept that a particle's and a mind's nature are both beginningless. In some cases we cannot explain this. It is just the nature of things, the way things are. Mind has cognitive power. Why? That's its nature! Matter has no cognitive power. Why? That's its nature. Living beings have an innate desire for happiness. Why? It's our nature!

Fabien: When you say mind and space particles are beginningless, does that mean they will always be there?

Dalai Lama: No. Beginningless does not mean eternal. Let me explain. A human life—a human body with a human mind—has a beginning. This human body started to form at a given moment, as did the human mind, which is connected to that body from the moment of conception. But both mind and body come from their own previous continuity. The body comes from the mother's egg and the father's sperm. Those parents in turn came from their parents through generations of ancestors. We can go back one billion years to jellyfish, and even further, to particles. These were not necessarily sentient beings, but they were living particles. And going further, before the big bang, we believe particles were already there. The original, substantial cause of this human body can be traced back to those particles.

Fabien: And the mind?

Dalai Lama: This body is connected with this universe. This mind is independent. It could have come from another universe….We can only explain the big bang theory in a way that is within our understanding. We cannot go beyond. As far as I know, the cosmologists today say there has only been one big bang. If they can prove that this is true, then Buddhist theory needs to be checked, because we say there are several. According to us, there was one big bang, the universe developed out of that, and then it disappeared into a black hole—or something like that. Things remained empty for some time. Then another big bang occurred.

Fabien: Is that the theory of *kalpa*, or cosmic eras?

Dalai Lama: One big bang cycle is longer than an eon, a kalpa. The span of time from the beginning of one big bang through its completion and the beginning of another big bang is a *kalchen*, or "great kalpa."

Fabien: Was there a first big bang?

Dalai Lama: Time is beginningless. My point is that in relation to a particular event—in this case, the conception of a human life with body and mind—one can say there is a beginning in time; but if you trace the substantial causes of both body and mind back to their origins, you cannot find a beginning.

Fabien: So according to Buddhism, everything has an explanation. There is no mystery.

Dalai Lama: Lord Buddha was exceptional. Apart from him, I think that not even our great saints like Milarepa would have been able to imagine or understand computers! You see, Buddhists can't necessarily explain everything.

Fabien: What I mean is this: in both material and metaphysical fields, you don't accept anything as mysterious. There always has to be some basis, correct?

Dalai Lama: That is what I'm trying to say. The Buddha could accomplish the enlightened mind because its very nature was already there. That is why buddhahood—enlightenment—is possible. If there were no such nature or potential, it would be impossible.

If you ask, "Why is time beginningless?" the answer is "That's its nature." If you decide to believe the opposite, then you get stuck in more complex and unsolvable questions. How did the first particle arise? If it is without a cause, then it is beyond the law of causality. Why should the first particle escape the laws of causality when all the others that follow don't? It doesn't fit. If you accept the idea of a creator, then the question is "Why did the creator create these things, and who created the creator?" Whether there is a beginning or not, it becomes very complicated.

Since we follow the path of reason, we prefer to accept the thesis that is the most logical, even it we cannot prove it completely. If you have two alternatives, one that you can't completely prove and another that you also can't prove and moreover results in more contradiction, logically you will choose the alternative that creates the least contradiction.

Fabien: What did the Buddha say about this question?

Dalai Lama: He said, "Samsara has no beginning and no end." When Buddha said, "Samsara has no beginning," it was not only from the point of view of ultimate truth, but also conventional truth. If samsara has no beginning, neither do the particles that compose it. If samsara had a beginning, then Buddha would also have had a beginning, and that would make things much more complicated.

Fabien: Is the question still open to debate?

Dalai Lama: Oh, yes, of course.

Fabien: Are there Buddhists who spend their life contemplating this?

Dalai Lama: No, not that question. Would that solve the problem of suffering? Anyway, our study in this field is not sufficient, but here is where the big difference between spiritual matters and science arises. Despite some similarities—in terms of the logic involved, for instance—they are totally different.

The spiritual aspect, for Buddhists, is that Buddha was enlightened. According to the Mahayana teachings, he attained enlightenment not in his lifetime as Siddhartha, the historical Buddha, but much earlier. That enlightened being came to India and started to preach according to his awakened experience. For us, the teachings did not come through an ordinary person's experiments that resulted in buddhahood. Buddha was someone who was already realized and started to teach. So we, his followers, accept those teachings. We do not have the capacity to add to this.

In the meantime—and this is very unique—we have the right and the freedom to question the Buddha's words. If some of his teachings appear to contradict our normal experience or our ordinary sensory perceptions, then we can question his words and use a different interpretation. Buddha himself gave us that liberty. Now nirvana and, beyond that, buddhahood, are dimensions that are very mysterious for us. It is extremely difficult with our present, conventional capacities as unenlightened beings to investigate or experiment with these dimensions. Although we cannot fathom such things, we can have some notions of them.

In a way, this process of spiritual understanding is similar to scientific method. In the beginning, scientists had only a rough idea about the moon or Mars. Their calculations were not precise. Now that they can reach these places, they can carry out detailed experiments. Similarly, buddhahood is difficult to explain precisely, but we can say that since we have a mind, the state of buddhahood can be achieved.

Likewise, our negative emotions have no sound basis. There is no logic supporting them. They are just negative emotions. However, positive emotions have a reason and a sound basis. For example, attachment arises for no reason, whereas compassion develops through reasoning, thinking, studying. We realize that others are just like us. I don't want pain, you can say to yourself, so other sentient beings don't want pain either. With this perspective, when we see someone suffering, we understand them and develop compassion. Sometimes when we feel strong compassion, it provokes a very powerful emotional response. Yet we can use reason to accept that feeling voluntarily. The moment we do so, we enjoy a kind of clarity. We have gotten closer to grasping our deeper mental nature. When there is only pain or suffering, it sometimes overwhelms our mental clarity, and we become dull. But when, out of compassion, we accept suffering voluntarily, suffering has a reason and a purpose. As a result, the powerful emotional responses that arise along with compassion do not destroy our basic mental strength.

Do you see the difference? By analyzing our daily experiences we can reduce our negative emotions and increase our positive emotions. Due to emptiness and because we possess buddha nature, we know that these negative emotions can be eliminated. The combination of all these reasons allows us to say, in a general way, that buddhahood is possible.

It is still very difficult to explain enlightenment precisely. We have to rely on the accounts of others to penetrate such advanced levels of philosophical and spiritual debate. Nevertheless, to accept such accounts we have to prove the value of the person who made these statements. Therefore, we study the Buddha's teachings on interdependence and other very profound theories. Once we are convinced he is truly authentic, there is no reason *not* to rely on him. He has no reason to lie.

Scientific knowledge is transmitted by ordinary beings. Their predecessors reached a certain point and transmitted their knowledge to the following generations, who continue to investigate on the basis of their findings. It's quite different than Buddhism in that sense.

Fabien: If I understand correctly, spiritual transmission from teacher to disciple is an important element of Buddhist teaching. The authentic experience of a master makes the teachings very clear.

Dalai Lama: That is what we call the "blessing lineage." There is some form of energy transmitted continuously from the Buddha himself. Qualified, genuine masters possess that energy and can pass it on to their disciples. This is mysterious! If a group of a hundred disciples receives the same teaching or initiation from the same teacher at the same time, only a few will receive the full transmission. Others will garner less benefit, some none. Still others, due to their negative thoughts toward the teacher, will not only deflect that positive energy, but will create more negative karma while listening to the teacher.

Fabien: Do love and compassion have a role to play in spiritual transmission? Are they essential?

Dalai Lama: Yes, this is very true. In the Mahayana or *Tantrayana* teachings, compassion is required on both sides: teacher and disciple. Of course, the lama is supposed to have more experience and a deeper realization than the disciple, but to transmit that special sacred energy he must have compassion. Otherwise, as the saying goes, it is just like trying to fill an empty vessel from another empty vessel.

Fabien: I would like to come back to the subject of Tibet. It seems that Tibet was once the country with the largest number of sages and learned religious teachers per capita. In Europe, America, or other places I don't think one could ever find so many wise persons, sages, or saints per square mile as in pre-Chinese Tibet.

Dalai Lama: Do you think so? It is true that the population of Tibet was very small, around six million people, before the Chinese occupation began. For such a small population, it does seem that the work accomplished in the field of Buddhist philosophy and spiritual training is very vast. Maybe Tibetans had no other subject to study, so those with good brains had only one possibility: the Buddhadharma.

By historical chance, Tibet is the only nation that received and preserved a complete form of the Buddhadharma. Sri Lanka and Burma are true Buddhist countries that had great masters for centuries. But these masters had no opportunity to study Mahayana and Tantrayana, and the local population rejected the concepts contained in these teachings. The Mahayana teachings flourished for a time in Indochina and China, but not in a complete form. Tibet is the only country where all levels of Buddhism were studied, practiced, and preserved. That does make it more authentic. Somehow—for some reason—we had that opportunity.

Fabien: Is it because the country was closed to outsiders for so long, therefore preventing external influences from damaging the transmission of the Dharma?

Dalai Lama: That is one aspect.

Fabien: Did it have anything to do with the place itself, the altitude?

Dalai Lama: That is possible. Perhaps some "mysterious forces" were also involved. I don't know why Tibet was so privileged. There must have been some strong karmic link with Buddha Shakyamuni and also Chenresig, my boss. Very compassionate, my boss! Hee, hee!

Fabien: Do you believe in ghosts, spirits of the dead?

Dalai Lama: Of course! Among mammals and other sentient beings who possess a body, we can see so many different species. Similarly, there are also many kinds of formless beings—that is, formless compared to us. From their perspective, they have a form.

Sometimes the Dalai Lama has a dual role: one in the Tibetan community, as a human being, and one in the ghost realm. You may have heard of Shugden, the controversial protector who has recently caused some problems among Tibetan communities. I have the great responsibility to fight with that spirit in the mysterious realms. So here is a case where a human being has a responsibility to interfere in the spirits' world! Ha!

I also have a very close connection with the Nechung oracle and the protectress of Tibet, Palden Lhamo. Isn't it strange? Anyhow, my personal experience has convinced me that there are many varieties of ghosts and many different kinds of spirits.

Anne: Are you convinced of this because you have seen them, or because of other signs?

Dalai Lama: I cannot see them. I am not a *migtongwa*, someone who has a special ability to see the spirits; but I do feel the presence of these mysterious forces. Just like human beings, some are positive and helpful, while others are harmful, and some are neutral.

Fabien: Do they live in a parallel world or in our world?

Dalai Lama: I think the ones I mentioned above live in the same world as we do. Some spirits may have their own worlds and visit our world to help human beings or to create problems for them.

Fabien: Are there also some elemental forces or beings that are linked to the environment, that feel responsible for nature?

Dalai Lama: Surely. In Tibet there are quite a number of cases where springs ran dry and trees shriveled up after the Cultural Revolution. Nowadays, when lamas go back and reopen temples and monasteries in these places, the springs come back to life. There have been several such cases. In the future, we could do research in this field.

Fabien: You know of Alexandra David Neel, the French explorer who spent many years in Tibet earlier this century. She wrote many books about the magic and mystery of Tibet. She spoke of black magic, of sorcerers wearing aprons made of bones, and so on. What is the origin of black and white magic in Tibet? Do they come from shamanistic or Bön sources that were then transmitted to Buddhism?

Dalai Lama: Bön, Tibet's traditional religion, is obviously now very much impregnated with Buddhist *Madhyamika* logic. Bönpo (followers of Bön) even took direct quotations from the great Indian Buddhist sage, Chandrakirti. I have noticed that in their debates they use the same arguments as the Sakya and the Gelug schools of Tibetan Buddhism, particularly on subjects such as logic, the *Prajnaparamita* (Perfection of Wisdom), and the Middle Path. These arguments are surely borrowed from Buddhism. If they had already existed in the Bön tradition, there would have been no need to import Buddhism from India. My conclusion is that before Buddhism flourished in Tibet there was a simple form of faith. This tradition continued to develop after Buddhism was introduced. Many aspects of Bön and Buddhism are quite similar, but there are also many differences. Bön practitioners circumambulate sacred places, like *chöten* (Tibetan reliquaries or cairns), in a counterclockwise fashion, while Buddhists always walk clockwise. Bönpos never use the word Dharma, they always use the word "Bön" when referring to spiritual teachings.

The magical rites you refer to come from Buddhism and are found mainly in the Tantrayana teachings. The bone ornaments and aprons you mentioned are used in certain tantric ceremonies. They are not normally related to black magic. But magic depends entirely on how one uses it. Used in the wrong way, it becomes black magic.

The main purpose of these "magic" techniques is to benefit sentient beings. For example, in the practices related to the Heruka and Kilaya tantras, we emanate many wrathful forms. Such practices have a definite purpose, which is very clearly defined. They are only to be used with infinite compassion and the realization of emptiness. A practitioner who has these capacities is qualified to perform such rites. If an unqualified person uses these mantra, rites, and *yantra* (ritual symbols), they can sometimes create problems for others. That is sad. Speaking honestly, used in the wrong way, some tantric texts become black magic. Because of this, the practice and transmission of Tantrayana is very strict. It is not for everyone.

Fabien: Is a teacher who transmits these techniques to an unworthy disciple responsible for the way they are used?

Dalai Lama: Yes. I know of a qualified teacher who used these techniques during his lifetime. At the end of his life he wrapped all these scriptures in a special cloth, which he sealed. No one, except an extremely qualified practitioner, is even allowed to see these documents.

Fabien: And yet the tantric tradition comes from the Buddha himself.

Dalai Lama: Correct, and I am a practitioner of tantric Buddhism! But the Tantrayana teachings are also transmitted through individuals. For example, when they were in states of deep meditation, masters such as Dilgo Khyentse Rinpoche and Dudjom Rinpoche, both of whom I have met many times, had clear visions of Padmasambhava, Vajradhara, and other deities. They received tantric teachings from these authentic masters of the lineage through visions. That Tantrayana transmission took place in the twentieth century, more than two thousand five hundred years after Buddha Shakyamuni passed away. Yet such lineages are authentic. The Padmasambhava who appeared in the visions of those great masters is the same being who came to Tibet in the eighth century to spread the Dharma. The *Vinaya* transmission is different. Monastic vows cannot be transmitted through a vision. Rather, the lineage must continue via an unbroken human lineage, beginning with the Buddha.

Fabien: There are other stories about Buddhist saints who never died, like Padmasambhava, who is said to have disappeared into the sky. Such beings seem more like divinities than saints to me.

Dalai Lama: As far as I know, there are four or five great saints who never died. You cannot see them, but, in special cases, people who have a karmic connection with them can meet them, even now. Vimalamitra is still alive in China, Mitrasugi lives in India, and the three vajra brothers of the Gelug tradition still reside in Tibet.

Fabien: On another subject, many heads of state use astrologers, mediums, or clairvoyants to help them rule their country. How do you consult the Nechung oracle?

Dalai Lama: In the same manner. Protectors such as the Nechung oracle took a life-long pledge in front of Guru Padmasambhava. They vowed to serve the Buddhadharma, to be responsible for its protection throughout the ages, and never to harm sentient beings. Unlike other controversial spirits, these protectors have taken the bodhisattva vow of true love and compassion. Even if I want to manipulate them, I can't.

So far, they have been very friendly to me, which tends to prove that I am quite honest. If I do something wrong, I suppose they will no longer be kind and supportive. Until now, whenever we meet they treat me as their master. In the future, I don't know.

Fabien: How important is astrology to you?

Dalai Lama: It is not important.

Fabien: Even Tibetan astrology?

Dalai Lama: No.

Fabien: But astrology is used in Tibetan medicine.

Dalai Lama: I believe in Tibetan medicine, but I don't think it relies on astrological provisions.

Fabien: Then what use is astrology?

Dalai Lama: In Lhasa, the medical college and the astrological institute were associated, as they are here in Dharamsala. On one occasion, when I visited the Dharamsala Tibetan Medical and Astrological Institute (TMAI), I told the students I was convinced Tibetan medicine had a great future ahead of it and encouraged comparative studies between our medical system and other systems. As for astrology, I said quite frankly that I had no faith in it. Apparently, the students were quite disheartened and subsequently questioned the value of the institute. So the following year I repeated my statement, specifying that it was just my personal opinion. I did not mean that our astrological system was not an important part of Tibetan culture, and stressed that they should persevere in their studies.

Anne: Aren't certain astrological texts connected to sacred medical texts?

Dalai Lama: Not in the usual way people view astrology. The Tantrayana texts, seen in light of ordinary people's concepts, sometimes mention that certain retreats should start on specific days. But the Buddha said that whatever happens to you is due to your karma, your actions, and causality. He never said it was due to *kar-ma*—the Tibetan word for stars.

Anne: But when you refer to the full moon or the new moon—specifically, that certain days of the lunar cycle are good days for practice and purification—is that not related to the influence of the stars and planets?

Dalai Lama: This practice is due to the relation between planets, physical elements, and constituents of the human body. For people who have faith in such things they are important, so they will perform certain practices on certain days according to their belief. It doesn't concern Buddhism as a whole—at least I don't think so.

Fabien: Do you see the color of people's auras?

Dalai Lama: No, I know nothing about this subject.

Fabien: But you've heard about it?

Dalai Lama: Oh yes, I've even seen photos of auras around the hands, for instance.

Fabien: So it is not a Tibetan system?

Dalai Lama: I have never heard of auras in a Buddhist context. It may have something to do with merit or fortune. Beings with powerful merit are naturally surrounded by a kind of subtle magnificence. The aura might be connected to that. Beings with good karma might have more aura, and those who are unlucky or unfortunate, less. Have you noticed how some people, despite a good education, a good brain, and everything else, always get caught in unlucky situations? Yet some people who are not so capable are always lucky.

Fabien: Your Holiness, do you have a spiritual teacher?

Dalai Lama: Of course! I can count fifteen teachers, up to now.

Fabien: Do you still work with all of them?

Dalai Lama: Most of them have passed away, but five or six are still alive. And in the future, in Tibet, I may have more teachers—qualified ones, not volunteers! I know that some people take advantage of an interview with me to say they are my teacher when they are back in Tibet. It can be very useful for them. But when I appear in photos with these people, you can see whether I am happy and smiling, or, on the contrary, reserved. That is an indication of the role they play in my spiritual practice.

So I have had many strange experiences because of my position as Dalai Lama! If I remained hidden in the mountains, all these problems would never exist, and I could be a good practitioner.

Fabien: Of what does your daily practice consist?

Dalai Lama: These days, when I am in Dharamsala, I wake up at 3:30 in the morning. Then—it has become automatic—I start reciting some mantra to bless the voice. After that I recite various other mantras. Then I do some long-life practice, mainly the transmissions I received from Dilgo Khyentse Rinpoche, Trulshig Rinpoche, and Chogye Trichen Rinpoche. These are deity practices with Tara, Tsepakme, and so on. Then I chant some other mantra. Then, until about 5:15, I do guru yoga practice with Lopon Rinpoche (Padmasambhava) and Je Rinpoche (Tsongkhapa, founder of the Gelug school of Tibetan Buddhism) and I recite *sung gnag* and *chegnag.* These are different sutras and mantras that help remove sickness and obstacles.

Then I have breakfast, during which I like to read something. I also like to listen to the Tibetan program on Voice of America. As soon as breakfast is over, I start another guru yoga and do some meditation on bodhicitta and shunyata, after which I do deity yoga with about eight different mandala. Too many! All that lasts until 8:30 or 9:00.

I spend the rest of the morning either working in my office or reading some philosophical texts. I have lunch at noon. For about two years now, I have vegetarian food one day, non-vegetarian the next. That way, at least six months of the year I am a vegetarian. I can not give up meat completely. I did try for two years in 1965, but then I got hepatitis B. I later found out it was quite a serious form, and I still have some liver problems as a result of this illness.

In the afternoon I always come to this room. If it is Sunday and there are no audiences, I sometimes invite a few old people to come and describe their life in Tibet before 1959. It makes me feel happy to talk to these ex-officials, old lamas, and scholars.

I have tea at six in the evening. As a Buddhist monk I don't take dinner. We are not supposed to eat solid food after the sun crosses the meridian. If I feel very hungry, then I eat a few biscuits, with salutations to the Buddha, thinking, "The Dalai Lama's health is more important." Ha, ha! I think the Buddha is really so kind, isn't he? He has such a broad vision, he can accept that the Dalai Lama needs to eat biscuits sometimes!

Until eight or so, I make some offerings to the protectors, such as Mahakala and Palden Lhamo. Then I sleep from 8:30 to 3:30, in one fell swoop.

Fabien: What do you dream about?

Dalai Lama: Nothing unusual. A few days ago I dreamt I was in Tibet, surrounded by the Chinese. I was very anxious, wondering how to escape. I woke up and rejoiced to find myself in India, free!

Actually, I have no faith in dreams, neither mine nor those of other people, but sometimes one has exceptional dreams. In one of these I saw my previous incarnation, the Indian sage Drupchen Nagpopa, a great master of the Heruka lineage. I have always been very fond of a certain statue of Heruka that I've had since childhood. Later, someone told me that statue had belonged to this great Indian sage. We are somehow connected.

The late Taklung Shaptrung once told me that, when he was giving some Taklung teachings to the late Dilgo Khyentse Rinpoche, he actually saw all the lineage lamas vividly appear on the walls of the temple in Nepal. He was just explaining this very casually, but while I was listening to him these teachings really came alive for me.

Another time I had a very vivid dream about a high lama. One day in my dream an abbot from Drepung Monastery said, "Jamyang Choje (the head of that monastery) has not yet come." At that moment I thought, "I am Jamyang Choje," but my name was different. I felt that I was supposed to be called Samyepa. In the dream I thought it was better not to tell the abbot about this. So I answered, "He may come later." The next day when I met Ling Rinpoche, who was still alive at that time, I told him my dream. He said, "Jamyang Choje was sometimes called Samyepa, because he was born in Samye." I had no previous knowledge of that. My tutor patted me on the back and congratulated me. That dream made me think there may have been some connection between that lama and me. In terms of ultimate reality, however, Jamyang Choje was a great master. I'm just a petty person compared to him. I really don't want to hint that I am anything great or a reincarnation of such and such a teacher. If that were my intention, my bhikshu vow might be damaged. But I do sometimes feel I've had certain extraordinary experiences that might be of use to my close friends in developing conviction.

Fabien: I would like to ask you about shunyata, or emptiness. In the nineteenth century this concept was incorrectly understood and translated in the West as "nothingness." People thought Buddhism was nihilistic.

Dalai Lama: That was wrong.

Fabien: Sure, but many people, including the pope, continue to think of Buddhism in this way. Can you explain emptiness in a few words?

Dalai Lama: Yesterday you referred to the space in which compassion grows. Sometimes emptiness is like that space. It is not space *in itself,* but it acts as the space that allows all functions to arise. If absolute cohesiveness were present, then nothing could change, and all the laws of causality could not function. My hand could not move. But everything is moving, which indicates that there is some kind of empty space. In fact, it is the absence of independent existence—another term for emptiness—that allows all things to function.

Fabien: Scientists say that inside the electron there is almost nothing: one-third matter and two-thirds empty space. A quark is just a mathematical point. We cannot see it or find it. We know that particles are made of electrons and that we are made of particles. Therefore, two-thirds of anything material is emptiness. So modern science seems to lean toward proving that emptiness is a reality and not just a nihilistic view of existence.

Dalai Lama: Emptiness and matter are two sides of the same coin. However, the term emptiness is used differently according to different texts. According to the Madhyamika texts, shunyata implies dependent arising or interdependence. In the trekchö level of the higher Dzogchen and Mahamudra tantra, it implies the clear light mind, or luminosity. Although there are two explanations of emptiness—one connected to the Madhyamika or sutra, and the other to the tantra— they are related. They are simply different aspects of the same thing.

In Dzogchen, *katag* or primordial purity is the emptiness aspect, while *lhundrup* or spontaneous arising is the interdependent aspect. At this level shunyata specifically means "the clear light as a basis of all." These very profound views have nothing to do with nihilism.

Fabien: For a philosophy of such metaphysical depth I am intrigued by the immense respect Buddhists show to sacred objects. Jewish people say that to prostrate oneself before a statue or an image is idolatry. What is the Buddhists' attitude to images?

Dalai Lama: In Buddhism, the scriptures say that when one has deeper realization, one should not prostrate oneself before statues or circumambulate holy objects. The very purpose of doing these things is to achieve realization. If a person is fully realized, then there is no need to act in this manner. It is better to meditate on that realization than to do prostrations. But for anyone else, it is better to bow than not to bow. At least you will remind yourself of the goal you are pursuing!

The object itself is not precious—its value lies in what it represents. When we do prostrations, we are supposed to imagine that the statue placed in front of us conjures up the true essence of buddhahood. If we don't, what's the use?

We also make no distinction between a statue made of gold or of clay. We should not put a golden Buddha higher and a clay one lower, and we cannot put a simple protector's statue, even if it be made of gold, higher than a Buddha statue, even if the latter is made of clay. What matters is what the statue represents for us.

Fabien: I have another question about suffering. I find it strange that Buddhists reflect so much on suffering and yet are always very joyful. Where does that joy come from? How can we develop that?

Dalai Lama: I don't think Buddha ever advised us to meditate just on suffering and its causes, without also reflecting on the cessation of suffering and the path to that cessation. The Four Noble Truths—suffering, the cause of suffering, its cessation, the path to cessation—go together. To realize that there are causes that produce suffering and that it is also possible for these sufferings to cease makes our mind fresh and helps to develop a firm determination to achieve the cessation of all suffering. Just meditating on the first two truths—suffering and its cause—without considering the two latter ones would not help. Better to drink some alcohol and forget about suffering! The last two truths reveal that, not only can suffering be ended, but there is an efficient way to achieve this state. When these last two aspects are clear, reflecting on suffering becomes worthwhile.

Fabien: So the idea is not just to accept suffering as something unavoidable?

Dalai Lama: No, not at all. Take the example of war. Look at what is happening in Bosnia. Nobody knows how to end the problem, everyone hesitates, and it continues endlessly. If we know the causes, if we know we can use certain methods to solve the problem, then we can tackle war with confidence, determination, and joy. But if we haven't an inkling of what the outcome will be, it is very difficult to move. Is that clear?

If, in the midst of suffering, we know there is a possibility of it ending and are aware of the means to make that happen, we develop the confidence necessary to overcome that suffering.

Fabien: On your altar here there are two statues. We already spoke about Guru Padmasambhava. Can you tell us about Avalokiteshvara, your "boss," as you mentioned earlier.

Dalai Lama: Avalokiteshvara is called "Chenresig" in Tibetan. We also call him "Thukje Chenbo," the Greatly Compassionate One. He took the vow to help all sentient beings, not just human beings.

Fabien: I heard that Chenresig wanted to free each sentient being from suffering. One day the task seemed too immense, and he got discouraged. His heart exploded out of sorrow, and he appeared with eleven heads and a thousand arms, emanating myriad divinities. Do you ever lose hope? Where do you find the courage to continue, to practice, to serve beings, to be the Dalai Lama, with all the responsibility you hold? In which part of your being do you find this motivation?

Dalai Lama: Chenresig is so serious. I'm not like that. In fact I think that strength comes to me through training with verses from Shantideva, such as: "As long as space remains, as long as there are suffering beings, I will remain to serve." This vow and the practice it underlines are very strong. They give me inner strength. For me, the purpose of life is happiness, or satisfaction, the true source of which is helping and serving others. Then life becomes something meaningful. One day when the first Dalai Lama was quite old, he said to his disciples, "Now I am too old, it is time to go."

"Do you mean you are about to go to some heaven?" asked a disciple.

"Heaven? Not at all. My main desire is to be reborn wherever there is the most suffering," said the Dalai Lama. These words return to my mind over and over again. That attitude is truly wonderful. It gives one a real purpose. Otherwise, just to go to some heaven and get drunk on some celestial alcohol, with some great rock music and everything—

Hee, hee! It's more or less the same, isn't it?

Fabien: That's a risky bet. So you are never tempted to give up?

Dalai Lama: Never. Wherever I go—France, Germany, America, Africa, or Australia—I receive a very good response from people. I feel that the goodness in humanity responds to that attitude. If I am sincere, if I respect people, then they are receptive and respond accordingly. This gives me encouragement. Even the small birds and insects trust me if I feed them and treat them with gentleness.

The story of Chenresig is authentic, but it is a symbol. It is impossible for a genuine bodhisattva to give up. Another version of this same story says that he was in fact already enlightened, but manifested that form when his head split open. Then Amitabha blessed him and increased his power to help beings. What a beautiful inspiration!

Fabien: Maybe it means that Chenresig had tremendous capacities that he was not yet using and his apparent discouragement was a way to catalyze all those capacities.

Dalai Lama: That's right. It multiplied his energy.

Fabien: That is why the bodhisattva vow is so beautiful. It is so powerful that just the thought of giving it up could make Chenresig explode into many compassionate forms. How incredible. Do you have to keep refueling this motivation?

Dalai Lama: Definitely. Every day. That is the bodhicitta practice. I usually spend several minutes reflecting on Shantideva's verses and trying to shape my mind. These days I think my mind has become very stupid. Previously, when I would reflect on certain verses that refer to the compassionate mind and try to mould my motivation with altruism, I would often cry. I really felt something every morning. That feeling of compassion remained with me all day long. Months and years went by like that. Such a practice has given great meaning to my life. Sometimes I might look foolish. So what?

Epilogue

As we left His Holiness' residence my eyes were shining, and the elation that I felt made the ground seem somehow light and buoyant under my feet. Three glasses of champagne could not have simulated the feeling I had when I emerged from the Dalai Lama's presence. A meal at a nearby restaurant brought me back down to more earthly concerns. The smell of diesel fuel and the sounds of car horns and goats bleating as they were loaded onto the bus with the passengers were all part of the pleasure with which I ate my tandoori chicken. But the pandemonium of the marketplace just outside could not drown out His Holiness' deep voice and contagious laughter still singing in my head like music. It swelled as I left the restaurant and made my way back to the hotel.

My discussions with His Holiness had challenged my Judeo-Christian discomfort and guilt about money and my notion of money as evil. With a few precise gestures of his powerful hands, His Holiness had put money back in its true place, as just one of the components of happiness, in fourth place after peace of mind, health, and friendship.

To be content with a harmonious mixture of these four aspects appeared to me to be the correct attitude to life. I was relieved to know that His Holiness considered money important and capable of creating much well-being, yet not indispensable.

His Holiness had a disarmingly easy way of opening up my perspectives and dissolving my conceptual barriers. For instance, I had always made a huge effort to be "spontaneous," which for me meant analyzing myself and learning to be at home with myself and with others. Now, suddenly, it seemed that all the work I had put into being spontaneous was only a small portion of my journey. Simply feeling at one with myself and the world wasn't enough, for it did not guarantee that compassion would take seed and flourish inside of me.

Meeting His Holiness was for me a powerful assurance that the ideals of compassion and love that he speaks about are more than idle theories. He is a living, breathing testament to the effectiveness of the path he teaches. He has a vast sense of personal responsibility, but it is never heavy or constricting. Instead he seems to be thoroughly suffused with joy, curiosity, and a wonderful sense of humor, and I could not help but feel enveloped within it.

Back at the hotel, I sat on the veranda and ruminated on the events of the past week. The trickling of a small waterfall brought me back to the present. The sound of the ceaseless running of the water made me think of the blood coursing through my body. As long as we live, as long as our hearts beat and our lungs breathe, the potential for enlightenment is there, and nothing and no one can deprive us of it. By training ourselves to become more and more aware, with altruism as our foundation, we can join His Holiness in the ocean of enlightened love.

Appendix

GLOBAL COMMUNITY AND THE NEED FOR UNIVERSAL RESPONSIBILITY

The Global Community

As the twentieth century draws to a close, we find that the world has grown smaller and the world's people have become almost one community. Political and military alliances have created large multinational groups, industry and international trade have produced a global economy, and worldwide communications are eliminating ancient barriers of distance, language, and race. We are also being drawn together by the grave problems we face: overpopulation, dwindling natural resources, and an environmental crisis that threatens our air, water, and trees, along with the vast number of beautiful life forms that are the very foundation of existence on this small planet we share.

I believe that to meet the challenge of our times, human beings will have to develop a greater sense of universal responsibility. Each of us must learn to work not just for his or her own self, family, or nation, but for the benefit of all humankind. Universal responsibility is the real key to human survival. It is the best foundation for world peace, the equitable use of natural resources, and through concern for future generations, the proper care of the environment.

For some time, I have been thinking about how to increase our sense of mutual responsibility and the altruistic motive from which it derives. Briefly, I would like to offer my thoughts.

One Human Family

Whether we like it or not, we have all been born on this earth as part of one great human family. Rich or poor, educated or uneducated, belonging to one nation or another, to one religion or another, adhering to this ideology or that, ultimately each of us is just a human being like everyone else: we all desire happiness and do not want suffering. Furthermore, each of us has an equal right to pursue these goals. Today's world requires that we accept the oneness of humanity. In the past, isolated communities could afford to think of one another as fundamentally separate and even existed in total isolation. Nowadays, however, events in one part of the world eventually affect the entire planet. Therefore we have to treat each major local problem as a global concern from the moment it begins. We can no longer invoke the national, racial or ideological barriers that separate us without destructive repercussions. In the context of our new interdependence, considering the interests of others is clearly the best form of self-interest.

I view this fact as a source of hope. The necessity for cooperation can only strengthen humankind, because it helps us recognize that the most secure foundation for the new world order is not simply broader political and economic alliances, but rather each individual's genuine practice of love and compassion. For a better, happier, more stable and civilized future, each of us must develop a sincere, warm-hearted feeling of brother- and sisterhood.

The Medicine of Altruism

In Tibet we say that many illnesses can be cured by the one medicine of love and compassion. These qualities are the ultimate source of human happiness, and our need for them lies at the very core of our being. Unfortunately, love and compassion have been omitted from too many spheres of social interaction for too long. Usually confined to family and home, their practice in public life is considered impractical, even naive. This is tragic. In my view, the practice of compassion is not just a symptom of unrealistic idealism but the most effective way to pursue the best interests of others as well our own. The more we—as a nation, a group or as individuals—depend upon others, the more it is in our own best interests to ensure their well-being.

Practicing altruism is the real source of compromise and cooperation—merely recognizing our need for harmony is not enough. A mind committed to compassion is like an overflowing reservoir—a constant source of energy, determination, and kindness. This mind is like a seed—when cultivated, it gives rise to many other good qualities, such as forgiveness, tolerance, inner strength, and the confidence to overcome fear and insecurity. The compassionate mind is like an elixir—it is capable of transforming bad situations into beneficial ones. Therefore we should not limit our expressions of love and compassion to our family and friends. Nor is compassion only the responsibility of clergy, health care professionals, and social workers. It is the necessary business of every part of the human community.

Whether a conflict lies in the field of politics, business, or religion, an altruistic approach is frequently the sole means of resolving it. Sometimes the very concepts we use to mediate a dispute are themselves the cause of the problem. At such times, when a resolution seems impossible, both sides should recall the basic human nature that unites them. This will help break the impasse and, in the long run, make it easier for everyone to attain their goal. Although neither side may be fully satisfied, if both make concessions, at the very least the danger of further conflict will be averted. We all know that this form of compromise is the most effective way of solving problems—why, then, do we not use it more often?

When I consider the lack of cooperation in human society, I can only conclude that it stems from ignorance of our interdependent nature. I am often moved by the example of small insects, such as bees. The laws of nature dictate that bees work together in order to survive. As a result, they possess an instinctive sense of social responsibility. They have no constitution, laws, police, religion, or moral training, but because of their nature they labor faithfully together. Occasionally they may fight, but in general the whole colony survives on the basis of cooperation. Human beings, on the other hand, have constitutions, vast legal systems, and police forces; we have religion, remarkable intelligence, and a heart with a great capacity to love. But despite our many extraordinary qualities, in actual practice we lag behind those small insects. In some ways, I feel we are poorer than the bees.

For instance, millions of people live together in large cities all over the world, but despite this proximity, many are lonely. Some do not have even one human being with whom to share their deepest feelings, and live in a state of perpetual agitation. This is very sad. We are not solitary animals that associate only in order to mate. If we were, why would we build large cities and towns? But even though we are social animals compelled to live together, we unfortunately lack a sense of responsibility toward our fellow humans. Does the fault lie in our social architecture—the basic structures of family and community that support our society? Is it in our external facilities—our machines, science and technology? I do not think so.

I believe that despite the rapid advances made by civilization in this century, the most immediate cause of our present dilemma is our undue emphasis on material development alone. We have become so engrossed in its pursuit that, without even knowing it, we have neglected to foster the most basic human needs of love, kindness, cooperation, and caring. If we do not know someone or find another reason for not feeling connected with a particular individual or group, we simply ignore them. But the development of human society is based entirely on people helping each other. Once we have lost the essential humanity that is our foundation, what is the point of pursuing only material improvement?

To me, it is clear: a genuine sense of responsibility can result only if we develop compassion. Only a spontaneous feeling of empathy for others can really motivate us to act on their behalf. I have explained how to cultivate compassion elsewhere. For the remainder of this short piece, I would like to discuss how our present global situation can be improved by greater reliance on universal responsibility.

Universal Responsibility

First, I should mention that I do not believe in creating movements or espousing ideologies. Nor do I like the practice of establishing an organization to promote a particular idea, which implies that one group of people alone is responsible for the attainment of that goal, while everybody else is exempt. In our present circumstances, none of us can afford to assume that somebody else will solve our problems; each of us must take his or her own share of universal responsibility. In this way, as the number of concerned, responsible individuals grows, tens, hundreds, thousands, or even hundreds of thousands of such people will greatly improve the general atmosphere. Positive change does not come quickly and demands ongoing effort. If we become discouraged, we may not attain even the simplest goals. With constant, determined application, we can accomplish even the most difficult objectives.

Adopting an attitude of universal responsibility is essentially a personal matter. The real test of compassion is not what we say in abstract discussions but how we conduct ourselves in daily life. Still, certain fundamental views are basic to the practice of altruism.

Though no system of government is perfect, democracy is that which is closest to humanity's essential nature. Hence those of us who enjoy it must continue to fight for all people's right to do so.

Furthermore, democracy is the only stable foundation upon which a global political structure can be built. To work as one, we must respect the right of all peoples and nations to maintain their own distinctive character and values.

In particular, a tremendous effort will be required to bring compassion into the realm of international business. Economic inequality, especially that between developed and developing nations, remains the greatest source of suffering on this planet. Even though they will lose money in the short term, large multinational corporations must curtail their exploitation of poor nations. Tapping the few precious resources such countries possess simply to fuel consumerism in the developed world is disastrous; if it continues unchecked, eventually we shall all suffer. Strengthening weak, undiversified economies is a far wiser policy for promoting both political and economic stability. As idealistic as it may sound, altruism, not just competition and the desire for wealth, should be a driving force in business.

We also need to renew our commitment to human values in the field of modern science. Though the main purpose of science is to learn more about reality, another of its goals is to improve the quality of life. Without altruistic motivation, scientists cannot distinguish between beneficial technologies and the merely expedient. The environmental damage surrounding us is the most obvious example of the result of this confusion, but proper motivation may be even more relevant in governing how we handle the extraordinary new array of biological techniques with which we can now manipulate the subtle structures of life itself. If we do not base our every action on an ethical foundation, we run the risk of inflicting terrible harm on the delicate matrix of life.

Nor are the religions of the world exempt from this responsibility. The purpose of religion is not to build beautiful churches or temples but to cultivate positive human qualities such as tolerance, generosity, and love. Every world religion, no matter what its philosophical view, is founded first and foremost on the precept that we must reduce our selfishness and serve others. Unfortunately, sometimes religion itself causes more quarrels than it solves. Practitioners of different faiths should realize that each religious tradition has immense intrinsic value and the means for providing mental and spiritual health. One religion, like a single type of food, cannot satisfy everybody. According to their varying mental dispositions, some people benefit from one kind of teaching, others from another. Each faith has the ability to produce fine, warmhearted people and despite their espousal of often contradictory philosophies, all religions have succeeded in doing so. Thus there is no reason to engage in divisive religious bigotry and intolerance, and every reason to cherish and respect all forms of spiritual practice.

Certainly, the most important field in which to sow the seeds of greater altruism is international relations. In the past few years the world has changed dramatically. I think we would all agree that the end of the Cold War and the collapse of communism in Eastern Europe and the former Soviet Union have ushered in a new historical era. At the end of the 1990s it would seem that human experience in the twentieth century has come full circle.

This has been the most painful period in human history, a time when, because of the vast increase in the destructive power of weapons, more people have suffered from and died by violence than ever before. Furthermore, we have witnessed an almost terminal competition between the fundamental ideologies that have always torn the human community: force and raw power on the one hand, and freedom, pluralism, individual rights, and democracy on the other. I believe that the results of this great competition are now clear. Though the good human spirit of peace, freedom, and democracy still faces many forms of tyranny and evil, it is nevertheless an unmistakable fact that the vast majority of people everywhere want it to triumph. Thus the tragedies of our time have not been entirely without benefit, and have in many cases been the very means by which the human mind has been opened. The collapse of communism demonstrates this.

Although communism espoused many noble ideals, including altruism, the attempt by its governing elites to dictate their views has proved disastrous. These governments went to tremendous lengths to control the entire flow of information through their societies and to structure their education systems so that their citizens would work for the common good. Although rigid organization may have been necessary in the beginning to destroy previously oppressive regimes, once that goal was fulfilled, the organization had very little to contribute toward building a useful human community. Communism failed utterly because it relied on force to promote its beliefs. Ultimately, human nature was unable to sustain the suffering it produced.

Brute force, no matter how strongly applied, can never subdue the basic human desire for freedom. The hundreds of thousands of people who marched in the cities of Eastern Europe proved this. They simply expressed the human need for freedom and democracy. It was very moving. Their demands had nothing whatsoever to do with some new ideology; these people simply spoke from their hearts, sharing their desire for freedom, demonstrating that it stems from the core of human nature. Freedom, in fact, is the very source of creativity for both individuals and society. It is not enough, as communist systems have assumed, merely to provide people with food, shelter, and clothing. If we have all these things but lack the precious air of liberty to sustain our deeper nature, we are only half human; we are like animals who are content just to satisfy their physical needs.

I feel that the peaceful revolutions in the former Soviet Union and Eastern Europe have taught us many great lessons. One is the value of truth. People do not like to be bullied, cheated, or lied to by either an individual or a system. Such acts are contrary to the essential human spirit. Therefore, even though those who practice deception and use force may achieve considerable short-term success, eventually they will be overthrown.

On the other hand, everyone appreciates truth, and respect for it is really in our blood. Truth is the best guarantor and the real foundation of freedom and democracy. It does not matter whether you are weak or strong or whether your cause has many or few adherents, truth will still prevail. The fact that the successful freedom movements of 1989 and after have been based on the true expression of people's most basic feelings is a valuable reminder that truth itself is still seriously lacking in much of our political life. Especially in the conduct of international relations we pay very little respect to truth. Inevitably, weaker nations are manipulated and oppressed by stronger ones, just as the weaker sections of most societies suffer at the hands of the more affluent and powerful. Though in the past the simple expression of truth has usually been dismissed as unrealistic, these last few years have proved that it is an immense force in the human mind and, as a result, in the shaping of history.

A second great lesson from Eastern Europe has been that of peaceful change. In the past, enslaved peoples often resorted to violence in their struggle to be free. Now, following in the footsteps of Mahatma Gandhi and Martin Luther King, Jr., these peaceful revolutions offer future generations a wonderful example of successful, nonviolent change. When in the future major changes in society again become necessary, our descendants will be able to look back on the present time as a paradigm of peaceful struggle, a real success story of unprecedented scale, involving more than a dozen nations and hundreds of millions of people. Moreover, recent events have shown that the desire for both peace and freedom lies at the most fundamental level of human nature and that violence is its complete antithesis.

Before considering what kind of global order would serve us best in the post-Cold War period, I think it is vital to address the question of violence, whose elimination at every level is the necessary foundation for world peace and the ultimate goal of any international order.

Nonviolence and International Order

Every day the media reports incidents of terrorism, crime, and aggression. I have never been to a country where tragic stories of death and bloodshed did not fill the newspapers and airwaves. Such reporting has become almost an addiction for journalists and their audiences alike. But the overwhelming majority of the human race does not behave destructively—very few of the five billion people on this planet actually commit acts of violence. Most of us prefer to be as peaceful as possible.

Basically, we all cherish tranquillity, even those of us given to violence. For instance, when spring comes, the days grow longer, there is more sunshine, the grass and trees come alive, and everything is very fresh. People feel happy. In autumn, one leaf falls, then another, then all the beautiful flowers die until we are surrounded by bare, naked plants. We do not feel so joyful. Why is this? Because deep down, we desire constructive, fruitful growth and dislike things collapsing, dying, or being destroyed. Every destructive action goes against our basic nature; building, being constructive is the human way.

I am sure everybody agrees that we need to overcome violence, but if we are to eliminate it completely, we should first analyze whether or not it has any value.

If we address this question from a strictly practical perspective, we find that on certain occasions violence indeed appears useful. One can solve a problem quickly with force. At the same time, however, such success is often at the expense of the rights and welfare of others. As a result, even though one problem has been solved, the seed of another has been planted.

On the other hand, if one's cause is supported by sound reasoning, there is no point in using violence. It is those who have no motive other than selfish desire and who cannot achieve their goal through logical reasoning who rely on force. Even when family and friends disagree, those with valid reasons can cite them one after the other and argue their case point by point, whereas those with little rational support soon fall prey to anger. Thus anger is not a sign of strength but one of weakness.

Ultimately, it is important to examine one's own motivation and that of one's opponent. There are many kinds of violence and nonviolence, but one cannot distinguish them from external factors alone. If one's motivation is negative, the action it produces is, in the deepest sense, violent, even though it may appear to be smooth and gentle. Conversely, if one's motivation is sincere and positive but the circumstances require harsh behavior, essentially one is practicing nonviolence. No matter what the case may be, I feel that a compassionate concern for the benefit of others—not simply for oneself—is the sole justification for the use of force.

The genuine practice of nonviolence is still somewhat experimental on our planet, but its pursuit, based on love and understanding, is sacred. If this experiment succeeds, it can open the way to a far more peaceful world in the next century.

I have heard the occasional Westerner maintain that long-term Gandhian struggles employing nonviolent passive resistance do not suit everybody and that such courses of action are more natural in the East. Because Westerners are active, they tend to seek immediate results in all situations, even at the cost of their lives. This approach, I believe, is not always beneficial. But surely the practice of nonviolence suits us all. It simply calls for determination. Even though the freedom movements of Eastern Europe reached their goals quickly, nonviolent protest by its very nature usually requires patience.

In this regard, I pray that, despite the brutality of their suppression and the difficulty of the struggle they face, those involved in China's democracy movement will always remain peaceful. I am confident they will. Although the majority of the young Chinese students involved were born and raised under an especially harsh form of communism, during the spring of 1989 they spontaneously practiced Mahatma Gandhi's strategy of passive resistance. This is remarkable and clearly shows that ultimately all human beings want to pursue the path of peace, no matter how much they have been indoctrinated.

The reality of war

Of course, war and the large military establishments are the greatest sources of violence in the world. Whether their purpose is defensive or offensive, these vast powerful organizations exist solely to kill human beings. We should think carefully about the reality of war. Most of us have been conditioned to regard military combat as exciting and glamorous—an opportunity for men to prove their competence and courage. Since armies are legal, we feel that war is acceptable; in general, people don't feel that war is criminal or that accepting it is a criminal attitude. In fact, we have been brainwashed. War is neither glamorous nor attractive. It is monstrous. Its very nature is one of tragedy and suffering.

War is like a fire in the human community, one whose fuel is living beings. I find this analogy especially appropriate and useful. Modern warfare is waged primarily with different forms of fire, but we are so conditioned to see it as thrilling that we talk about this or that marvelous weapon as a remarkable piece of technology without remembering that, if it is actually used, it will burn living people. War also strongly resembles a fire in the way it spreads. If one area gets weak, the commanding officer sends in reinforcements. This is like throwing live people onto a fire. But because we have been brainwashed to think this way, we do not consider the suffering of individual soldiers. No soldier wants to be wounded or die; none of his loved ones wants any harm to come to him. If one soldier is killed, or maimed for life, at least another five or ten people—his relatives and friends—suffer as well. We should all be horrified by the extent of this tragedy, but we are too confused.

Frankly, as a child, I too was attracted to the military. Their uniforms looked so smart and beautiful. But that is exactly how the seduction begins. Children start playing games that will one day lead them into trouble. There are plenty of exciting games to play and costumes to wear other than those based on the killing of human beings. Again, if we as adults were not so fascinated by war, we would clearly see that to allow our children to become habituated to war games is extremely unfortunate. Some former soldiers have told me that when they shot their first person they felt uncomfortable, but as they continued to kill it began to feel quite normal. In time, we can get used to anything.

It is not only during times of war that military establishments are destructive. By their very design, they are the single greatest violators of human rights, and it is the soldiers themselves who suffer most consistently from their abuse. After the officers in charge have given beautiful explanations about the importance of the army, its discipline, and the need to conquer the enemy, the rights of the great mass of soldiers are almost entirely taken away. They are then compelled to forfeit their individual will, and, in the end, to sacrifice their lives. Moreover, once an army has become a powerful force, there is every risk that it will destroy the happiness of its own country.

There are people with destructive intentions in every society, and the temptation to gain command over an organization capable of fulfilling their desires can become overwhelming. But no matter how malevolent or evil are the many murderous dictators who currently oppress their nations and cause international problems, it is obvious that they cannot harm others or destroy countless human lives if they don't have a military organization accepted and condoned by society. As long as there are powerful armies, there will always be the danger of dictatorship. If we really believe dictatorship to be a despicable and destructive form of government, then we must recognize that the existence of a powerful military establishment is one of its main causes.

Militarism is also very expensive. Pursuing peace through military strength places a tremendously wasteful burden on society. Governments spend vast sums on increasingly intricate weapons when, in fact, nobody really wants to use them. Not only money but also valuable energy and human intelligence are squandered, while all that increases is fear.

I want to make it clear, however, that although I am deeply opposed to war, I am not advocating appeasement. It is often necessary to take a strong stand to counter unjust aggression. For instance, it is plain to all of us that the Second World War was entirely justified. It "saved civilization" from the tyranny of Nazi Germany, as Winston Churchill so aptly put it. In my view, the Korean War was also just, since it gave South Korea the chance of gradually developing a democracy. But we can only judge whether or not a conflict was vindicated on moral grounds with hindsight. For example, we can now see that during the Cold War, the principle of nuclear deterrence had a certain value. Nevertheless, it is very difficult to assess all such matters with any degree of accuracy. War is violence and violence is unpredictable. Therefore, it is far better to avoid it if possible, and never to presume that we know beforehand whether the outcome of a particular war will be beneficial or not.

For instance, in the case of the Cold War, though deterrence may have helped promote stability, it did not create genuine peace. The last forty years in Europe have seen merely the absence of war, which has not been real peace but a facsimile founded on fear. At best, building arms to maintain peace serves only as a temporary measure. As long as adversaries do not trust each other, any number of factors can upset the balance of power. Lasting peace can be secured only on the basis of genuine trust.

Disarmament for world peace

Throughout history, mankind has pursued peace one way or another. Is it too optimistic to imagine that world peace may finally be within our grasp? I do not believe that there has been an increase in the amount of people's hatred, only in their ability to manifest it in vastly destructive weapons. On the other hand, bearing witness to the tragic evidence of the mass slaughter caused by such weapons in our century has given us the opportunity to control war. To do so, it is clear we must disarm.

Disarmament can occur only within the context of new political and economic relationships. Before we consider this issue in detail, it is worth imagining the kind of peace process from which we would benefit most. This is fairly self-evident. First we should work on eliminating nuclear weapons, next, biological and chemical ones, then offensive arms, and, finally, defensive ones. At the same time, to safeguard the peace, we should start developing in one or more global regions an international police force made up of an equal number of members from each nation under a collective command. Eventually this force would cover the whole world.

Because the dual process of disarmament and development of a joint force would be both multilateral and democratic, the right of the majority to criticize or even intervene in the event of one nation violating the basic rules would be ensured. Moreover, with all large armies eliminated and all conflicts such as border disputes subject to the control of the joint international force, large and small nations would be truly equal. Such reforms would result in a stable international environment.

Of course, the immense financial dividend reaped from the cessation of arms production would also provide a fantastic windfall for global development. Today the nations of the world spend trillions of dollars annually on upkeep of the military. Can you imagine how many hospital beds, schools and homes this money could fund? In addition, as I mentioned above, the awesome proportion of scarce resources squandered on military development not only prevents the elimination of poverty, illiteracy and disease, but also requires the sacrifice of precious human intelligence. Our scientists are extremely bright. Why should their brilliance be wasted on such dreadful endeavors when it could be used for positive global development?

The great deserts of the world such as the Sahara and the Gobi could be cultivated to increase food production and ease overcrowding. Many countries now face years of severe drought. New, less expensive methods of desalinization could be developed to render sea water suitable for human consumption and other uses. There are many pressing issues in the fields of energy and health to which our scientists could more usefully address themselves. Since the world economy would grow more rapidly as a result of their efforts, they could even be paid more! Our planet is blessed with vast natural treasures. If we use them properly, beginning with the elimination of militarism and war, truly every human being will be able to live a wealthy well-cared for life.

Naturally global peace cannot occur all at once. Since conditions around the world are so varied, its spread will have to be incremental. But there is no reason why it cannot begin in one region and then spread gradually from one continent to another.

I would like to propose that regional communities like the European Community be established as an integral part of the more peaceful world we are trying to create. Looking at the post-Cold War environment objectively, such communities are plainly the most natural and desirable components of a new world order. As we can see, the almost gravitational pull of our growing interdependence necessitates new, more cooperative structures. The European Community is pioneering the way in this endeavor, negotiating the delicate balance between economic, military and political collectivity on the one hand and the sovereign rights of member states on the other. I am greatly inspired by this work. I also believe that the new Commonwealth of Independent States is grappling with similar issues and that the seeds of such a community are already present in the minds of many of its constituent republics. In this context, I would briefly like to talk about the future of both my own country, Tibet, and China.

Like the former Soviet Union, Communist China is a multinational state, artificially constructed under the impetus of an expansionist ideology and up to now administered by force in colonial fashion. A peaceful, prosperous and above all politically stable future for China lies in its successfully fulfilling not only its own people's wishes for a more open, democratic system, but also those of its eighty million so-called "national minorities" who want to regain their freedom. For real happiness to return to the heart of Asia— home to one-fifth of the human race—a pluralistic, democratic, mutually cooperative community of sovereign states must replace what is currently called the People's Republic of China. Of course, such a community need not be limited to those presently under Chinese Communist domination, such as Tibetans, Mongols and Urghurs. The people of Hong Kong, those seeking an independent Taiwan, and even those suffering under other communist governments in North Korea, Vietnam, Laos and Cambodia might also be interested in building an Asian Community. However, it is especially urgent that those ruled by the Chinese Communists consider doing so. Properly pursued, it could help save China from violent dissolution, regionalism and a return to the chaotic turmoil that has so afflicted this great nation throughout the twentieth century. Currently China's political life is so polarized that there is every reason to fear an early recurrence of bloodshed and tragedy. Each of us—every member of the world community—has a moral responsibility to help avert the immense suffering that civil strife would bring to China's vast population.

I believe that the very process of dialogue, moderation and compromise involved in building a community of Asian states would itself give real hope of peaceful evolution to a new order in China. From the very start, the member states of such a community might agree to decide its defense and international relations policies together. There would be many opportunities for cooperation. The critical point is that we find a peaceful, nonviolent way for the forces of freedom, democracy and moderation to emerge successfully from the current atmosphere of unjust repression.

Zones of Peace

I see Tibet's role in such an Asian Community as what I have previously called a "Zone of Peace": a neutral, demilitarized sanctuary where weapons are forbidden and the people live in harmony with nature. This is not merely a dream—it is precisely the way Tibetans tried to live for over a thousand years before our country was invaded. As everybody knows, in Tibet all forms of wildlife were strictly protected in accordance with Buddhist principles. Also, for at least the last three hundred years, we had no proper army. Tibet gave up the waging of war as an instrument of national policy in the sixth and seventh centuries, after the reign of our three great religious kings.

Returning to the relationship between developing regional communities and the task of disarmament, I would like to suggest that the "heart" of each community could be one or more nations that have decided to become zones of peace, areas from which military forces are prohibited. This, again, is not just a dream. Four decades ago, in December 1948, Costa Rica disbanded its army. Recently, 37 percent of the Swiss population voted to disband their military. The new government of Czechoslovakia has decided to stop the manufacture and export of all weapons. If its people so choose, a nation can take radical steps to change its very nature.

Zones of peace within regional communities would serve as oases of stability. While paying their fair share of the costs of any collective force created by the community as a whole, these zones of peace would be the forerunners and beacons of an entirely peaceful world and would be exempt from engaging in any conflict. If regional communities do develop in Asia, South America, and Africa, and disarmament progresses so that an international force from all regions is created, these zones of peace will be able to expand, spreading tranquillity as they grow.

We do not need to think that we are planning for the far distant future when we consider this or any other proposal for a new, more politically, economically and militarily cooperative world. For instance, the newly invigorated forty-eight member Conference on Security and Cooperation in Europe has already laid the foundation for an alliance between not only the nations of Eastern and Western Europe but also between the nations of the Commonwealth of Independent States and the United States. These remarkable events have virtually eliminated the danger of a major war between these two superpowers.

I have not included the United Nations in this discussion of the present era because both its critical role in helping create a better world and its great potential for doing so are so well known. By definition, the United Nations must be in the very middle of whatever major changes occur. However, it may need to amend its structure for the future. I have always had the greatest hopes for the United Nations, and with no criticism intended, I would like simply to point out that the post-World War II climate under which its charter was conceived has changed. With that change has come the opportunity to further democratize the UN, especially the somewhat exclusive Security Council with its five permanent members, which should be made more representative.

In Conclusion

I would like to conclude by stating that, in general, I feel optimistic about the future. Some recent trends portend our great potential for a better world. As late as the fifties and sixties, people believed that war was an inevitable condition of mankind. The Cold War, in particular, reinforced the notion that opposing political systems could only clash, not compete or even collaborate. Few now hold this view. Today, people all over the planet are genuinely concerned about world peace. They are far less interested in propounding ideology and far more committed to coexistence. These are very positive developments.

Also, for thousands of years people believed that only an authoritarian organization employing rigid disciplinary methods could govern human society. However, people have an innate desire for freedom and democracy, and these two forces have been in conflict. Today, it is clear which has won. The emergence of non violent "people's power" movements have shown indisputably that the human race can neither tolerate nor function properly under the rule of tyranny. This recognition represents remarkable progress.

Another hopeful development is the growing compatibility between science and religion. Throughout the nineteenth century and for much of our own, people have been profoundly confused by the conflict between these apparently contradictory world views. Today, physics, biology and psychology have reached such sophisticated levels that many researchers are starting to ask the most profound questions about the ultimate nature of the universe and life, the same questions that are of prime interest to religions. Thus there is real potential for a more unified view. In particular, it seems that a new concept of mind and matter is emerging. The East has been more concerned with understanding the mind, the West with understanding matter. Now that the two have met, these spiritual and material views of life may become more harmonized.

The rapid changes in our attitude towards the earth are also a source of hope. As recently as ten or fifteen years ago, we thoughtlessly consumed its resources, as if there was no end to them. Now, not only individuals but governments as well are seeking a new ecological order. I often joke that the moon and stars look beautiful, but if any of us tried to live on them, we would be miserable. This blue planet of ours is the most delightful habitat we know. Its life is our life; its future, our future. And though I do not believe that the Earth itself is a sentient being, it does indeed act as our mother, and, like children, we are dependent upon her. Now mother nature is telling us to cooperate. In the face of such global problems as the greenhouse effect and the deterioration of the ozone layer, individual organizations and single nations are helpless. Unless we all work together, no solution will be found. Our mother is teaching us a lesson in universal responsibility.

I think we can say that, because of the lessons we have begun to learn, the next century will be friendlier, more harmonious, and less harmful. Compassion, the seed of peace, will be able to flourish. I am very hopeful. At the same time, I believe that every individual has a responsibility to help guide our global family in the right direction. Good wishes alone are not enough; we have to assume responsibility. Large human movements spring from individual human initiatives. If you feel that you cannot have much of an effect, the next person may also become discouraged and a great opportunity will have been lost. On the other hand, each of us can inspire others simply by working to develop our own altruistic motivation.

I am sure that many honest, sincere people all over the world already hold the views that I have mentioned here. Unfortunately, nobody listens to them. Although my voice may go unheeded as well, I thought that I should try to speak on their behalf. Of course, some people may feel that it is very presumptuous for the Dalai Lama to write in this way. But, since I received the Nobel Peace Prize, I feel I have a responsibility to do so. If I just took the Nobel money and spent it however I liked, it would look as if the only reason I had spoken all those nice words in the past was to get this prize! However, now that I have received it, I must repay the honor by continuing to advocate the views that I have always expressed.

I, for one, truly believe that individuals can make a difference in society. Since periods of great change such as the present one come so rarely in human history, it is up to each of us to make the best use of our time to help create a happier world.

Glossary

arhatship. Nirvana that is beyond suffering, but which is not total enlightenment.

awakening. Synonym of enlightenment.

bhikshu. Fully ordained Buddhist monk.

bhumi. *See* ten bodhisattva levels.

bodhicitta. Literally the mind of enlightenment. On the relative level it is the wish to become a buddha in order to lead all beings to enlightenment and the basic motivation behind all Mahayana practice. On the absolute level it is direct insight into the ultimately empty nature of mind and phenomena.

bodhisattva. A being who has decided to bring all beings to enlightenment and is following the path of enlightenment. A sublime bodhisattva is one who has attained one of the ten bodhisattva levels.

Bön. The religious traditions prevailing in Tibet prior to the introduction of Buddhism. Bön is still practiced today.

Bönpo. A follower of the Bön religious tradition.

buddha. One who is enlightened. One who has dispelled the darkness of the two obscurations (of negative emotions and conceptual views) and developed the two kinds of omniscience (knowing the nature of phenomena and knowing the multiplicity of phenomena).

Buddha Shakyamuni. The historical Buddha, born as Siddhartha of the Shakya clan in India two thousand five hundred years ago.

Buddhadharma. *See* Dharma.

Chenresig (Sanskrit *Avalokiteshvara*). The bodhisattva embodying the compassion of all the buddhas. The Dalai Lama is believed by his people to be an incarnation of Chenresig.

chöten. Also known as a stupa. A physical structure, often containing relics, representing the thought plane of Buddha Shakyamuni. There are eight styles of chöten corresponding to eight important events in the life of the Buddha.

deity yoga. A Vajrayana practice centered on a deity that represents one's own potential for enlightenment. The deity can be male or female, peaceful or wrathful, and is chosen according to the practitioner's nature. Deity yoga is a swift means to transform one's ordinary, deluded perceptions into wisdom.

Dharma. This term has many different meanings. In the present context, it is synonymous with Buddhadharma and designates all the teachings of the Buddha, the buddhas, and the enlightened masters. According to Buddhist tradition, these teachings reveal the path to awakening. The Dharma has two main aspects: the transmission Dharma, that is, the words that serve as a support for the teachings; and the Dharma of spiritual realization resulting from authentic spiritual practice.

Dharma protectors. Wisdom protectors are emanations of buddhas or bodhisattvas who manifest in this form to protect the Dharma and the practitioners. Other Dharma protectors include spirits, gods, or demons subjugated by great realized beings and bound to oath to protect the Dharma.

Dilgo Khyentse Rinpoche (1910–1991). One of the greatest Tibetan masters of the twentieth century, holder of the lineages of all four major schools of Tibetan Buddhism. Student of, and master to, the present Dalai Lama; *see The Spirit of Tibet,* by Matthieu Ricard.

Dudjom Rinpoche (1904–1987). A great scholar and treasure discoverer of the Nyingma School of Tibetan Buddhism. One of his major works has been translated into English under the title *The Nyingma School of Tibetan Buddhism: Its Fundamentals and History.*

Dzogchen. The Great Perfection teachings. *Dzogchen* reveals the most direct approach to the essence of mind.

eightfold path. The fourth noble truth: right view, right intention, right speech, right action, right livelihood, right effort, right mindfulness, and right meditative concentration.

emotions (negative, conflicting, or afflictive; Sanskrit *klesha*). Mental phenomena that assail the body and mind and lead to harmful actions, creating a state of mental torment.

emptiness (or voidness). The realization of emptiness is a key practice of Mahayana Buddhism.

Gelug. One of the four major schools of Tibetan Buddhism. This school stems from the teachings of Tsongkhapa.

geshe. Literally a "spiritual friend." The title "geshe" designates a doctorate of philosophy in the monastic system.

guru yoga. Practice focused on actualizing one's teacher's realizations in one's own mind.

Heruka. A tantric deity that represents our ultimate nature. *He* is space (void), *ka* is wisdom, and *ru* the union of both.

interdependence. Generally speaking, Buddhist philosophy is based on interconnections. Nothing exists independently. Every phenomenon has a cause, and our actions and reactions produce, reinforce, or transform the effects that we experience in the future. The law of cause and effect is perpetuated by twelve interdependent factors that imprison beings in samsara, the wheel of existence. Ignorance produces mental formations that form consciousness, which gives birth to name and form, the origin of the six senses. These give rise to contact, which creates feelings (sensation) that awaken desire, which becomes grasping. Grasping turns into the drive to exist, which leads to birth and, consequently, old age and death. The necessary and sufficient condition leading to release from samsara is the destruction of any one of the twelve links in this chain.

Kagyu. One of the four major schools of Tibetan Buddhism. There are two major Kagyu traditions, the Marpa and Shangpa.

Kalachakra. Literally "wheel of time." A profound set of initiations and practices of the tantric tradition.

kalpa. Extremely great unit of space-time particular to South Asian cosmology.

Kalu Rinpoche (1904–1989). Great master and yogi of the Shangpa Kagyu tradition.

karma. A fundamental principle of Indian religions based on the conception of human life as a link in a chain of lives, each life being determined by acts accomplished in a previous life.

Karmapa. Name of a series of great lamas of the Marpa Kagyu School of Tibetan Buddhism. In the text, His Holiness is referring to the sixteenth Karmapa (1923–1981).

khandroma (Sanskrit *dakini*). Female spiritual helpers and adepts. Can refer generally to the feminine principle associated with wisdom. Ordinary khandromas have a certain degree of spiritual power, while wisdom khandromas are fully realized.

lama (Sanskrit *guru*). Literally "heavy" or "loaded" (with qualities). Designates a person who is capable of leading others to spiritual realization; teacher.

Madhyamika. Middle Way teaching on emptiness first expounded by Nagarjuna. "Middle" means that it is beyond the extremes of nihilism and eternalism.

Mahamudra. The Great Seal, meaning that the seal of absolute nature is on everything. This term can denote the teaching of Mahamudra or its realization.

Mahayana. The Great Vehicle, or the vehicle of the bodhisattvas. It is great because its aim is full buddhahood for all beings.

mandala. In the context of tantric practice, this refers to the universe with the palace of the deity at its center; in the context of an offering, it symbolizes the entire universe, which one offers up in gratitude for receiving Buddhist teachings.

mantra. Literally "that which protects the mind" (of the Vajrayana practitioner against all manifestations of ignorance). Generally refers to syllables whose incantation is a fundamental element of Vajrayana practice.

Milarepa (1040–1123). Tibet's great yogi and poet, whose biography and songs are among the best loved works of Tibetan Buddhism.

mind. In the Tibetan Buddhist context, the mind is not a real entity but a succession of moments of consciousness that we perceive as a continuity. The ultimate nature of the mind has two inseparable aspects: emptiness *(shunyata),* its essence; and luminosity, the nature of its cognitive faculties.

Nagarjuna (first–second century). Indian Buddhist master who expounded the *Madhyamaka* (Middle Way) teachings.

Naropa. Indian Buddhist master and teacher of Marpa, the founder of the Marpa Kagyu School of Tibetan Buddhism.

nirvana. The state of deliverance from suffering or samsara.

Nyingma. One of the four major schools of Tibetan Buddhism.

Padmasambhava (also known as Guru Rinpoche). Indian Buddhist scholar and tantric master who introduced Buddhism to Tibet in the eighth century.

powa. One of the six teachings of Naropa involving the transfer of consciousness at the moment of death. In Buddhism this practice is a preparation for the final hours through the realization of the illusory nature of all manifestations of samsara.

right. "That which results in happiness," according to Dudjom Rinpoche.

rinpoche. Literally "precious"; title given to recognized spiritual masters.

Sakya. One of the four major schools of Tibetan Buddhism.

samsara. The world of suffering and ignorance created by karma; also called cyclic existence.

Sangha. The community of Dharma practitioners, from ordinary beings to bodhisattvas.

Shantideva (seventh century). Indian sage and poet, author of *Bodhicaryavatara,* a treatise on bodhisattva practices in ten chapters. The Dalai Lama has given several commentaries (including *A Flash of Lightening in the Dark of the Night*) on this essential Mahayana guidebook.

sutra. A text containing the teachings of the Buddha.

tantra. Esoteric teachings of the Buddha, synonymous with Vajrayana and Mantrayana.

Tara. Feminine bodhisattva born from a tear shed by Chenresig. She represents the efficacy of enlightened compassion.

tathagatagarbha. Literally, "the essence of the buddha." Refers to the teaching that buddha nature is latent in all sentient beings.

ten bodhisattva levels (Sanskrit *bhumi*). The ten levels of realization reached by the bodhisattvas. These levels are far beyond ordinary beings.

thanka. Tibetan religious scroll painting.

Three Jewels. The Buddha, or Awakened One; the Dharma, or his teachings; and the Sangha, the virtuous community of practitioners. These three are the basis of Buddhist refuge. On a deeper level, Buddha represents our innate buddha nature, Dharma the natural purity of all phenomena, and Sangha the totality of all living beings.

Tilopa. One of the eighty-four great Buddhist sages of India, and Naropa's teacher.

trekchö, tögal. The two essential Dzogchen practices, through which primordial purity *(kadag)* and spontaneous arising *(lhundrup)* are revealed in the very midst of deluded thoughts and perceptions.

Tsepakme. Buddha of long life.

Tsongkhapa (1357–1419). Also called Je Rinpoche and Losang Drakpa, the founder of the Gelug School of Tibetan Buddhism.

tulku. Literally "manifestation body." In the experience of Tibetan Buddhists, a highly realized master is capable of maintaining control over his mind during the death process. He or she can decide where and when to take rebirth in order to continue serving beings.

tummo. One of the six teachings of Naropa, involving the production of vital heat through deep meditation.

Two Truths. Absolute, or ultimate, truth is that perceived through wisdom, without mental fabrications. According to Patrul Rinpoche, it is "beyond mind, unthinkable, inexpressible." Relative, or conventional, truth is the apparent truth perceived and taken as real by the deluded mind.

Vajradhara. In most schools, Vajradhara is the primordial Buddha at the beginning of the tantric lineages.

vehicle (Sanskrit *yana*). The Basic Vehicle, or Hinayana, is based on renunciation; the Great Vehicle, or Mahayana, is based on compassion; the Diamond Vehicle, or Vajrayana, is based on the tantras.

vinaya. The portion of the Buddhist canon containing the teachings on monastic discipline.

wisdom. The ability to understand correctly, usually with the particular sense of understanding emptiness.

wrong. According to Dudjom Rinpoche, "that which results in suffering." Anything that produces an unpleasant or painful effect.

yantra. Ritual symbol or design used in some Buddhist ceremonies.

Index

abortion, 44, 93–95
Africa and economic gap, 9
African medical systems, 104
aggression in fight for free Tibet, 72
alcohol, 6, 136
altruism
  in business, 146
  and economics, 43–63
  and international relations, 147
  medicine of, 142–45
  not at expense of oneself, 46
  on global scale, 44–45
  on individual scale, 45–46
Amitabha, 137
analysis of daily experiences, 123
animals
  and discernment, 35
  faculties of, 29
  and the law, 4
  rights of, 28–29
  and sexuality, 92
  Tibetan compassion for, 71
arms and demilitarization, 52
art, 101–2

Asian community, 157–58
astrology, 129–30
atheism, 72
attachment, 8, 31, 122
auras, 130
Avalokiteshvara (Chenresig), viii, 125,
  136–38

begging for alms, 8
beginningless nature of body and
  mind, 119–20
Benson, Dr. Herbert, 115
big bangs, multiple, 119–20
birth control, 10, 93
black magic, 126, 127
blessing lineage, 123
blood and suffering, 48–49
bodhicitta, 14, 138
bodhisattvas, 46, 57, 61, 138
Bön, 126, 127, 71
breast-feeding, 35
Buddha. See Shakyamuni Buddha
Buddhadharma. See also Buddhism,
  Dharma

its reasoned approach, 75
and science, 75
as sole study of Tibetans, 124
survival of, 61, 70–71
Tibet received full form of, 124
buddha nature, 80, 83–84
Buddhism. *See* also Buddhadharma,
    Dharma
and death, 109
and mind, 117
not for all of humanity, 75
and practice of other traditions, 67
and science, 75, 117, 122, 123
Buddhist culture, as distinguished
    from Buddhism, 71–72
business, and use of power, 15–16

causality, law of, 120, 134
Chandrakirti, 126
chastity, 60
Chenresig (Avalokiteshvara), viii, 125,
    136–38
children
becoming monks and nuns, 86
and exposure to death, 107–8
free expression of, 33
right conception and raising of, 44,
    85–86
right education of, 35–36, 78
and sex education, 92–93
China
and creation of a new political
    order, 157–58
defense against, 25
democratic movement in, 69,
    151–52
its government and Tibet, 68–69
Chirac, Jacques, 17
Christian Church, and ethics, 34
Christianity
and Creator, 68
and practice of other traditions,
    67–68
and reincarnation, 68

Churchill, Winston, 154
clear light, 115, 118, 134
Clinton, Bill, 16, 19
Cold War, 154, 159
Commonwealth of Independent
    States, 156, 159
communism, 3, 54, 147–48
community
global, 23–39
sangha as, 27–28
and support of the Dharma, 70
compassion
and betterment of the world, 33
development of, 122, 138
exists always as seed, 84
and international business, 146
Kalu Rinpoche as embodiment of,
    viii
and love, 31–32, 142–43
as means of happiness, 46–47
as means to reduce fear, 78
and mother's love, 31
and responsibility, 145
and sacred energy transmission, 124
competition, 27–28
compromise, 143
Conference on Security and
    Cooperation in Europe, 159
consciousness, 114
cooperation, in human society, 144
creativity, 101
creator, belief in, 67–68, 96, 120–21

Dalai Lama, Fifth, 101
Dalai Lama, First, 137
Dalai Lama, Fourteenth, Tenzin Gyatso
Chinese war against, 68–69
and creation of healing water, 116
daily practice of, 131–32
dreams of, 132–33
as emanation of Chenresig, viii
longevity of, 30, 69
and Nobel Peace Prize, 161
spiritual teachers of, 131

and Tibet, 20
David Neel, Alexandra, 126
death and dying, 105–9
death process, eight stages of, 109
deathlessness of saints, 128
death penalty, 99–100
debate, 88
demilitarization, 24–25, 52, 158–59
  See also disarmament
democracy
  as foundation of global political
    structure, 145–46, 160
  and laws, 3–4
  and voting, 16
Deng Xiao-ping, 18, 69
dependent arising. *See* interdependence,
  causality
desire
  undermines happiness, 39
  and the use of money, 8
devotion, blind, 59
Dharamsala, x, 44
Dharma, 5, 62. *See* also
  Buddhadharma, Buddhism
Dilgo Khyentse Rinpoche, 128, 131,
  133
disarmament, 154–55, 158–59
  See also demilitarization
disease
  Tibetan approach to, 102–3
  Western approach to, 79
divorce, 91
drugs, 77
Dudjom Rinpoche, 128
Dzogchen (Great Perfection), 114, 134

Eastern European freedom movements,
  148–49
ecology, 26, 50
  See also environment
economic gap
  between rich and poor countries,
    9–10, 146
  within countries, 9–10, 44

economics
  and altruism, 43–63
  and altruism at global level, 44–45
  and altruism at individual level,
    45–46
  bringing compassion into, 146
  creation of ethical code in world of,
    44
  and environmental issues, 45
education
  and birth control, 10
  both Tibetan and modern, 86–87
  and compassion, 33–34
  and dialectic debate, 88
  in free Tibet, 88
  integration of Buddhism into,
    86–87, 88
  sexual, 92–93
  and social environment, 87
elemental forces or beings, 126
emotions, negative, 122
emptiness, 75, 115, 116, 134
enlightenment
  difficulty of explaining, 123
  as potential, 84, 120
environment. *See also* ecology, pollution
  care for, 36–37
  and economic world, 45
  and the law, 4
  problems of, 50–51
ethics, code of, 34
  in business world, 44
euthanasia, 95
evolution, 38

faith, blind, 61
family, one human, 142
family planning, 93
five elements, 79, 102, 114, 118
Five Point Peace Plan, 68
flying, 114–15
food and monastic regulations, 8
four excellences, 5
Four Noble Truths, 37, 85, 135–36

freedom, 148, 160

Gabon, and economic gap, 9
Gandhi, Mahatma, 14
   non-violence of, 149, 150, 151
ghosts, 125
global
   awareness, 37–38
   community, 23–39
   warming, 50
Global Community and the Need for
   Universal Responsibility 23, 141–61
globalization, 44
God, 38, 58. *See also* Christianity
   and dependence, 80
   and ecumenism, 67–68
   and karma, 14, 96
   and money, 9
   and rebirth, 106
   and suffering, 96
   expectations of, 37
   grace of, 56
gold, touching of, 7
good companions, 5
good heart, development of, 34, 78
Green, Felix, 17
gross national product, 6, 10–11, 39, 53

happiness
   and insufficiency of material com-
     forts, 39
   and right action, 98
   worldly, 5
health, 5, 6, 102–3
Heruka tantra, 127
Hitler, Adolf, 84
human being, as the enemy, 48
human intelligence
   desensitizing of, 77
   and difference from other living
     beings, 29–30
   and solutions, 26
   as source of problems and fears,
     30–31, 77

wonderfulness of, 79
human nature
   as gentle and compassionate, 26, 33
   as sensible, 49

"Imagine All the People" (song), 19
India, poverty in, 6, 7
individual responsibility, 37
insects, and cooperation, 144
intelligence. *See* human intelligence
interdependence, 67–68.
   and legal systems, 3–4
   and mind, 117
   and miracles, 113–14
international council of sages, 24, 55
international police force, 155
internet, 90
inventions, 52
Israel
   and greening of landscape, 55
   and kibbutz, 54

jail, 98–99, 100
Jamyang Choje, 133
Jesus Christ, 37
Jewish tradition
   and concern for conversions to
     Buddhism, 58
   and microcosm and macrocosm, 37

Kalachakra teachings, 118
kalpas, 119–20
Kalu Rinpoche, vii–viii, 46, 67
Kangra, India, teacher training in,
   86–87
karma, 96–97
Karmapa, 18
katag (primordial purity), 134
khandroma (feminine deity), 113
kibbutz, 54
Kilaya tantra, 127
killing, Buddhist orientation to, 94–95
King, Martin Luther, 149
lama, 33, 59

laws, 3–4
leaders, global
   dialogue with, 17–18
   problems created by, 28
Lenin, Vladimir Ilyich, 14
Lennon, John, 18–19, 20
Ling Rinpoche, 133
"lost generation," 35, 48, 78, 84–85
love and compassion, 31–32, 142–43
luminosity, 134
lunar cycle and practice, 130

Madhyamika, and emptiness, 134
magical rites, 127
Maha Anuttara Yoga Tantra, 61
Mahamudra, 134
Mahayana, 57, 124
Mao Tse-tung, 13, 14, 53
marriage, 44, 91–92
Marxism
   critique of, 43
   and totalitarianism, 26
materialism and spirituality, 76
matter, 134
media
   and discussion of altruism, 51
   and power, 16
   and sensationalism, 90
   responsibility of, 50, 51, 79, 89–90
medical systems, 104–5
meditation
   and miraculous powers, 114–15
   on clear light, 115
   and peace of mind, 108
mercy killing, 95
migtongwa, 125
Milarepa, 115, 120
military establishments, 152–54
milk, 32, 49
mind, 5
   as beginningless, 119
   Buddhism begins with, 117
   committed to compassion, 143
miracles, 113–15

missionary zeal, 58
Mitrasugi, 128
monastic
   buildings, luxuriousness of, 62
   rules and ownership, 7
   training and "probation" period, 86
money, 4–6, 12
   and absence of magical powers, 5, 11
   and attachment, 8
   does not bring happiness, 39,
     45–46
   total amount produced insufficient,
     9, 11
   touching of, 7
motherhood, and compassion, 31–33
murder, 4, 15
music, 101
Muslims, 9, 104
   in Tibet, 71–72, 88

Nagarjuna, 75
Nagpopa, Drupchen, 132–33
Naropa, 59
national boundaries, disappearance of,
   54–55
Native Americans, comparison to
   Tibetans, 74
nature, humans as part of, 36.
   See also ecology, environment
Nechung oracle, 125
   and bodhisattva vow, 128–29
neutron bomb, 48, 49
nihilism and Buddhism, 133–34
nirvana, 5, 7–8
non-violence
   and international order, 150–52
   and Tibetan struggle, 68
northern countries and economic gap,
   9–10
nuclear weapons
   and economics, 45
   reduction of, 24, 26–27

optimism, 26

oracles and divination, 69–70, 125
oral traditions, 104
ordination, monastic, 7–8
orphans, 86

Padmasambhava, 69, 128, 131
pain and right action, 98
Palden Lhamo, 125
pardon, 99
parents and education of children,
    85–86
particles as beginningless, 119
peace, global, 154–56, 159–60
peace of mind, 5–6, 33, 78
    and death, 106
    and meditation, 108
plants, 91
pluralism, 57–59
politicians and spirituality, 18
pollution
    reduction of, 35, 36–37, 50
    See also environment
poultry farms, dismantling of, 30
powa (release of consciousness), 109
power
    and the law, 4
    and the media, 16
    and responsibility, 4, 14–16
    types of, 13
practice of multiple traditions, 67
prison system, 98–99, 100
proselytizing
    and following of one's own
        tradition, 57, 58
    as outdated concept, 59
prostrations, 135
Prozac, 77, 78, 79
psychokinesis, 116
public life, love and compassion in,
    142–43

Radio Here and Now, vii
rainbows, 113–14
rape, 4, 93

refuge, taking, viii
regional communities, 156
reincarnation
    and Christianity, 68
    and death, 106, 108
religion
    and individual freedom, 55–56
    and moral codes, 34
    non-necessity of, 34, 55–56
    not for all at this time, 75
    and universal responsibility,
        146–47
religious systems, and the law, 4
responsibility
    dependent on compassion, 145
    and the media, 50, 51, 79, 89–90
    universal, 141, 145–49
    and use of power, 14–15
"right desire," 8

sacred objects, 135
samsara, 121
sangha, 27–28
satisfaction, 5, 53
science
    and development of ethical code,
        34, 35
    as different than Buddhism, 123
    and economic motivations, 45
    human values in, 146
    its noticing of its own limits, 79
    and similarities to Buddhist
        approach, 75, 104, 117, 122
    and spirituality, 76, 79, 160
selfishness, and altruism, 46–47
sex
    and Buddhism, 60–61, 92
    change, 109
    and excessiveness, 92–93
sexual abuse, 60, 92
sexual scandals, 61, 62–63
Shakyamuni Buddha, viii, 37, 120
    and acknowledgement of different
        schools of Buddhism, 57

and astrology, 130
and connection to Tibet, 125
and giving of permission to
   question his words, 122
as previously enlightened being,
   121–22
and tantra, 128
Shantideva, 137, 138
shunyata (emptiness), 75, 115, 116,
   134
Siddhartha, 121. *See also* Shakyamuni
   Buddha
socialism, 26, 54
social work, 63
Sogyal Rinpoche, 105
Somalia, starvation in, 6
southern countries and economic gap,
   9–10
Soviet Union, collapse of, 26, 147
space, 118, 119, 134
spirituality
   internal and external, 56
   and science, 76, 79, 160
spiritual teachers, 33
   qualified, 59–60
   testing of, 61
   unqualified, 35–36
spirit world, 125–26
sports, 100–101
Stalin, Joseph, 13, 14
suffering
   always present nature of, 85
   ending of, 135–36
   meditation on, 135–36

taking refuge, viii
Taklung Shaptrung, 133
Tantrayana
   and compassion, 124
   and magical rites, 127
   and the twentieth century, 128
tathagatagarbha, 80
technology as false hope, 80
television, 88–89

Tenzin Chogyal, 107
Tenzin Geyche, xi
Tenzin Gyatso. *See* Dalai Lama,
   Fourteenth
theft, 4
Thekchen Choling, xi
Three Jewels, viii
Three Vajra Brothers, 128
Thukje Chenbo. *See* Chenresig
Tiananmen Square massacre, 69
Tibet
   aggressive fight for freedom, 72
   escape from, 5
   freedom and the Buddhadharma,
      70
   and full form of Buddhadharma,
      124
   internal conflict amongst its people,
      73–74
   plan for after self–rule, 73–74, 88
   present political situation, 68–73,
      75–76
Tibetan art, 101–2
Tibetan Book of Living and Dying, The,
   105
Tibetan Buddhist centers outside
   Tibet, 70
Tibetan culture
   and basic way of life, 71
   comparison with Native Americans,
      74
   and spirit of the people, 71, 72
Tibetan Medical and Astrological
   Institute (TMAI), 129
Tibetan medicine, 102–3, 104
Tihar Jail, 98
Tilopa, 59
time, 117–18, 120
Tito, Marshall, 73
tolerance
   for all religious traditions, 57–59,
      75, 147
   and Tibetan culture, 71
totalitarian regimes, 3, 26, 148

transmission, of sacred energy, 123–24
Trulshig Rinpoche, 131
Tsogtrug Rangdrol, 114
Tsongkhapa, 131
tulkus, 59, 60, 116
tummo, 115

unemployed, community of, 55
unemployment, attitudes toward,
    53, 54
United Nations, 23
   and nuclear disarmament, 24
   and support of altruism, 51
United States, 44, 159
universal responsibility, 141, 145–49

Vajradhara, 128
Vimalamitra, 128
Vinaya transmission, 128

violence, 150–51
   Buddhist view on, 94
   and television, 77
   and war, 152–54
Voice of America, 131
vows, monastic, 7–8, 60

war, 152–54
Western centers of Tibetan Buddhism,
   70
Western culture and external
   approach, 79
worldly happiness, 5
world organization for humanity,
   23–24
world peace, 20

Zhou Enlai, 17
Zone of Peace, 158

About the Contributors

Venerable Tenzin Gyatso, who describes himself as a "simple Buddhist monk," is widely recognized to be both the spiritual and the temporal leader of the Tibetan people. Known more popularly in the West as the Dalai Lama, he attained worldwide recognition in 1989 when he was awarded the Nobel Peace Prize for his dedication to a non-violent struggle for the liberation of Tibet. Speaking and writing eloquently on the need for a commitment to compassion and a sense of universal responsibility, the Fourteenth Dalai Lama travels extensively and frequently visits the Europe and North America.

Fabien Ouaki is the chairman and chief executive of the Tati group, which employs seventeen hundred people worldwide. Forty years old and father of four, he was drawn to Tibetan Buddhism after meeting Kalu Rinpoche fourteen years ago. In 1994 Fabien organized a forum on business and ethics in Paris, which included His Holiness the Dalai Lama. Fabien is convinced that human values can operate in the world of business and finance and that mutual interest and universal responsibility are essential for the economics of tomorrow. He may well be the archetype of the business leader of the third millennium.

Anne Benson, mother of two, was born in California in the 1950s and moved to France with her parents at age ten. At seventeen she traveled to India to meet and study with one of the greatest Tibetan masters of this century, Kyabje Kangyur Rinpoche. She assisted his son, Pema Wangyal Rinpoche, in setting up the Centre d'Etudes de Chanteloubre in the Dordogne, the European seat of both Dudjom Rinpoche and Dilgo Khyentse Rinpoche. After spending several years lobbying for His Holiness the Dalai Lama and the Tibetan cause, Anne now dedicates her time to translating Tibetan into French and English.

About Wisdom

Wisdom Publications, a not-for-profit publisher, is dedicated to making available authentic Buddhist works for the benefit of all. We publish translations of the sutras and tantras, commentaries and teachings of past and contemporary Buddhist masters, and original works by the world's leading Buddhist scholars. We publish our titles with the appreciation of Buddhism as a living philosophy and with the special commitment to preserve and transmit important works from all the major Buddhist traditions.

If you would like more information or a copy of our mail-order catalog, please contact us at:

Wisdom Publications
199 Elm Street
Somerville, Massachusetts 02144 USA
Telephone: (617) 776-7416
Fax: (617) 776-7841
Email: info@wisdompubs.org
Web Site: http://www.wisdompubs.org

The Wisdom Trust

As a not-for-profit publisher, Wisdom Publications is dedicated to the publication of fine Dharma books for the benefit of all sentient beings and dependent upon the kindness and generosity of sponsors in order to do so. If you would like to make a donation to Wisdom Publications, please do so through our Somerville office. If you would like to sponsor the publication of a book, please write or email us for more information. *Thank you.*

Wisdom Publications is a non-profit, charitable 501(c)(3) organization and a part of the Foundation for the Preservation of the Mahayana Tradition (FPMT).